Pope John Paul II, on his return to Rome after his visit to Ireland in 1979, commenting on the ruins of Clonmacnoise, was speaking prophetically I believe, when he said:

'These stones have yet a great mission to realise for the world.'

This book is a little treasure of practical spirituality. Drawing from the wisdom of the desert, the Celtic tradition and from contemporary contemplative guides, Sr Kathleen presents a Gospel vision that goes to the core of our Christian discipleship. Using the symbol of the tower she traces how we can experience even now the unfolding of the divine energy of the resurrection in our daily living. Walking the path of light marked out here will unwrap the heart to grace, unshackle the soul and transform lives.

Francis Cotter OFM, *author of* The Coming of the Friars Minor to Ireland, *and* Glimpses of the Franciscan Way.

I enjoyed reading it and have derived much from your insights into the topic. I thought that it was extremely well written, beautifully expressed and well argued. Your conclusions on the relationship of Cassian to the round tower are certainly an important contribution to the field, and deserve to be more widely known.

Author of The Irish Round Tower *(1999), Brian Lalor was General Editor of the internationally award-winning* The Encyclopaedia of Ireland *(2003).*

Kathleen Lynch FMDM

The Sublime Round Tower

An Iconic Call to Contemplative Prayer

First published in 2013 by
the columba press
55A Spruce Avenue, Stillorgan Industrial Park,
Blackrock, Co. Dublin

Cover by Shaun Gallagher
Origination by The Columba Press
Printed by ScandBook AB, Sweden

ISBN 978 1 78218 129 3

All Scripture quotations, including those occurring within Cassian's writings, are taken from *The New Jerusalem Bible*, London, DLT, 1985, unless otherwise stated.

All royalties from the sale of this book will be donated to the FMDM African Mission at the request of the author.

Contents

Acknowledgements

I would like to dedicate this work to the memory of my beloved parents. To my mother Margaret, for her example of lived discipleship. To my father Sean, for awakening in me a deep love for our Celtic heritage.

I want to acknowledge my debt of gratitude and esteem to Dr David L. Walker, former Bishop of Broken Bay diocese, NSW, Australia, for introducing me to the writings of John Cassian. I express my sincere thanks to Prof. Thomas O'Loughlin for his encouragement, sound advice and the foreword he has provided, and to Dr David Kelly OSA, who with kindness, patience and scholarly expertise has directed and supported me in the production of this work and who took time and care to proofread it for me. I also want to express my deepest appreciation to Mrs Madeleine Phillips for her gracious generosity and professional competence in typing the text. I am particularly grateful to Mr Brian Lalor for his time, interest and permission to use original photographs.

Finally I wish to express loving gratitude to my family and to my FMDM sisters for their love, support and encouragement.

Buíochas le Dia

List of Illustrations

The photographs are by courtesy of Mr Brian Lalor from his book *The Irish Round Towers, Origins and Architecture Explored.*

Which of you here, intending to build a tower, would not first sit down and work out the cost to see if one had enough to complete it? … So in the same way, none of you can be my disciple without giving up all that one owns.
(Lk 14:28–33)

Foreword

Christians are always caught in a moment between the future, towards which they journey in hope, and the past, which they draw their inspiration and their wisdom. When they lose sight of the future, faith becomes but an atavism, a worship of the past, or the quest from some half-remembered Utopia. In this scenario, the present and the future is threatening rather than inviting, and the call to build the kingdom is lost amidst a swirl of stale incense and pious images. It is in the future, at the end that Christians will find perfection, the fullness of understanding, and truth.

On the other hand, when they lose sight of the past – of the long history of Israel, or the life of Jesus and memories of his early disciples, and of their own history with its ups and downs – good and bad – then Christianity becomes just a philosophical system rather than a real way of life, a way of following, and a way of seeking goodness, truth and beauty. Christian discipleship is a journey rooted in the past but with the newness of the future always beckoning us.

Of course we often lose sight of one or other of these poles: the Alpha and Omega of Christian existence. In time when all seems to be going well for the churches they treat the past as simply 'prologue' and try to describe the future in systems; when things are apparently going hard for the churches they ignore the future and seek to reinvent the past.

This is the tension we see every Easter Vigil when the great candle celebrates the pasting moment by placing the year's date midway between A of the past, or origins, and history, and the Ω of the future, of new departures, of hope, and of the End.

Holding the balance between the past and the future is always a delicate task – and here Kathleen Lynch's book, this book, strikes the right note. She looks back to the past – the memories of the desert in John Cassian who was 'the bestseller' in the monasteries in early medieval Ireland – but she does so to point out the call of the future. She looks at those wonders of stonework – the great bell towers we call round towers – and sees them not as glimmers for the past but as beacons for the future. They remind us of the call to prayer, and prayer enables us to face the future. And facing into the future with hope it helps us to discover in every age and in every situation and in every person that God is already present.

Cassian saw himself as a historian who transformed a remembered past in the hot sands of Egypt and hills of Palestine into a vision of discipleship that could be lived out in the farmland and pastures of southern Gaul, and from there it would be further adapted for the wet woodland and windswept islands of Ireland. This book looks back to him, and those inspired by him, seeking energy for Christians today on their pilgrimage. The round towers so often used as emblems of an ancient past are reimagined as beacons as we travel into the third Christian millennium.

Thomas O'Loughlin
Professor of Historical Theology
University of Nottingham
A 2013 Ω

Introduction

Cassian: an Authentic Authority for Renewal in the Church

The round towers standing majestically in the heart of the ancient Irish monastic settlements have puzzled and challenged me from an early age. As my pilgrimage of life unfolded, I found myself in New Zealand. By an unplanned turn of events, an opportunity to read the writings of John Cassian (*c.*360–435) was offered to me by Bishop David Walker,[1] who was then the Director of the Education Centre for Christian Spirituality, Randwick, New South Wales, Australia. To my surprise and delight I discovered embedded in the writings a whole spirituality of Gospel living, leading to contemplative prayer, based on *Jesus' parable of the tower* (Lk 14:28–33). The wisdom of this teaching places Cassian as an authentic authority for renewal of the Church not only in Ireland but in the world.

The purpose of this book is to elucidate Cassian's teaching on the sublime tower as a framework for the spiritual journey, in the call and transforming power of prayer and to demonstrate persuasively that to the monastic communities the round tower was central to the meaning and purpose of their lives. This will be done with particular reference to Cassian's writings, the *Conferences* and the *Institutes.* We shall examine how Cassian uses Jesus' teaching on the tower to express his understanding of prayer in the journey of Christian discipleship, and how this teaching reached Ireland through St Patrick and the monks of Gaul. Cassian's teaching on the tower image portrays vividly yet concretely the inter-relationship between the preparation steps necessary for prayer and contemplative prayer itself, in the lived experience, not only for monks and nuns, who were members of lay communities, but for all would-be disciples. The relevance of his teaching can be aptly applied to the spiritual hunger of this twenty-first century and for the many people searching for a deeper personal and meaningful relationship with their God today.

I hope to evoke renewed interest in Cassian, as he excels in integrating, in a wonderful way, the lived experience of the spiritual journey, with the goal of all spiritual endeavours, namely the contemplation of God. In the emerging discipline of 'spirituality' today where there is considerable ambiguity regarding its content and definition,[2] Cassian's teaching is worth revisiting. I also wish to propose that Cassian's spiritual teaching on the 'tower image' is the key to the unlocking of the unresolved 'enigmatic' mystery of the Irish Round Tower.[3] I intend this work to seriously examine and claim that these sublime towers were designed and built as a visual representation of the predispositions required of discipleship in the call to prayer for all who seriously desire to follow Christ, leading to the experience of transforming communion in God, as they concurrently served as an environment of solitude for the anchorite, and excellent outlet for an audible bell call to prayer. In the light of Cassian's teaching, these 'towers' can awaken or reawaken Christians today and indeed all humankind, to the realisation of their full human potential in the ever-present challenge in prayer to transcend the 'false self' and journey towards the glorious destiny of 'becoming a new creation in Christ' (2 Co 5, 17).

Pope John Paul II, on his return to Rome after his visit to Ireland in 1979, was speaking prophetically, I believe, when commenting on the ruins of Clonmacnoise, that they had yet a great mission to realise for the world. I endorse that prediction, as I believe the sublime tower metaphor presents and unfolds the essential key for humankind today, to make that 'qualitative leap in the history of evolution and of life in general towards a new future life, towards a new world',[4] achieved for us through the Resurrection of Christ.[5] I welcome this opportune moment, to share my findings on these perennial icons of universal wisdom. To avoid repetition I am using the words image, icon, metaphor and symbol synonymously.

Our investigation will proceed through the following stages: the introduction will situate Cassian in his socio-cultural and historical context, and will establish the tower metaphor as a framework for the call to prayer in the spiritual journey. We will seek to elucidate Cassian's teaching on essential prerequisites for the foundational disposition of heart, necessary for this venture. We will then examine obstacles to the ongoing dynamic, in the conversion of life process, for building up 'the walls' through a virtuous lifestyle. This will be followed by an exploration into Cassian's insight into the reciprocal bond between one's lifestyle and the ongoing transformation through prayer into Trinitarian communion of God. In the light of historical evidence we will consider how Cassian's teaching came to impact on the monastic and eremitical life of the Church in

Ireland. Finally the application of this teaching will be presented for the spiritual journey today, in the light of the 'Universal Call' to holiness,[6] and the comparative findings in modern psychology so aptly brought to bear on Cassian's teaching, by Thomas Keating.[7]

Cassian's Writing: the First Summa of Spiritual Theology in the West.

There is a considerable amount of scholarly research on Cassian's life already in print. A succinct account is as follows: John Cassian, a monk and ascetical writer, was born in Scythia Minor *c.*AD360, and died in Marseilles in southern Gaul between AD432 and AD435. While still a youth, John was initiated into asceticism at a monastery in Bethlehem. In AD386 he undertook a trip to Egypt with his friend Germanus, where they encountered the monasticism of the desert monks and nuns. Toward AD399 or AD400 the two friends journeyed to Constantinople. There they met St John Chrysostom (*c.*AD347–407), by whom Cassian was ordained a deacon. As a priest, Cassian travelled to Marseilles in southern Gaul, where he founded two monasteries, one for men entitled SS. Peter and Victor and one for women under the title of St Savior.[8]

All three of Cassian's works *The Institutes* (*c.*AD417–18), *Conferences* (*c.*AD419–20) and *On the Incarnation of the Lord* (*c.*AD430): were written in Gaul,[9] at the request of Ecclesiastical pastors and have been preserved. A precise summary of their content and spiritual doctrine is stated here:

> The spiritual works of Cassian have a double merit. From the point of historical interest, they constitute the most

> interesting documents from monasticism in the 5th century. From a doctrinal point of view they form the first *summa* of spiritual theology in the West; and what is even more remarkable, the statements of the problems of spiritual life as they are exposed by Cassian in *The Institutes* and *Conferences* remain, with few variations, identical along the course of the history of Christian spirituality down to contemporary times.[10]

To fully appreciate Cassian as a sure guide for the spiritual journey, it is necessary to situate him in his historical context. In this way, one can gain a fuller appreciation of his Christology and Spirituality within his limited but sound psychological teaching. In his historical context he stood alongside St Augustine (*c.*AD354–430) as one of the principal figures in the Latin Church between (*c.*AD425–30).[11] He was familiar with the writings of the great Christian thinkers who had gathered in Egypt at the end of the second century to reflect on Christian religious experiences in a way unknown before. The 'Life of Antony' written by Athanasius (*c.*AD296–373) became an inspiration and challenge to the whole church.

Faith leaders and thinkers including Basil (*c.*AD330–79) and Evagrius of Pontus (*c.*AD345–99) from the East, with St Jerome (*c.*AD341–420) and Cassian from the West came to share in this extraordinary outpouring of faith. Evagrius was the one who provided a spiritual framework from the 'spirituality of the desert', which he drew principally from Origen (*c.*AD185–254).[12] Basil took it to the East, whilst Cassian took it to the West. Although revered in the East as a saint, it was in the West that Cassian was considered a great authority on the spiritual life and has been a great influence on the spiritual teaching tradition in the Western Church, by being 'incorporated' into the Benedictine Rule. Since this rule conquered Western monasticism, Cassian accompanied its diffusion. The foundations of his great influence had been laid.[13]

His Spirituality is Essentially Biblical

Cassian's spirituality is essentially biblical. He draws abundantly from Scripture and uses them only as one who had meditated on and prayed them can. Meeting Christ in biblical text was the goal of one who read, meditated and prayed over the Bible. He writes, one ought 'never to consent to open the gate of perfection, except to those who desired it with all faithfulness, and sought it with all sorrow of heart',[14] as this could have detrimental consequences for both disciple and teacher.

While Cassian shows that he was familiar with the work of individual Christian writers, namely Jerome, Basil, John Chrysostom, and although the framework for the spiritual journey was received from Evagrius, it was out of his own lived experience that he formed his teaching within this framework. To Cassian, spirituality could be likened to art. His reader should not just initiate the practice but learn the principles and apply these to one's own journey. This important teaching which is reiterated in many different ways, is Scripture-based: 'Forgetting all that lies behind me, and straining forward towards the finishing-point to win the prize of God's heavenly call upward in Christ Jesus' (Ph 3:13, 14).[15]

Cassian taught that the immediate aim, of the spiritual life was 'purity of heart, and that this should be the fundamental concern of the would-be disciple. The ultimate goal was the experience of the kingdom in contemplative prayer.[16] This would be given, but it was God's prerogative. 'The gift freely given by God is eternal life in Christ Jesus our Lord' (Rm 6:23). So like a good archer it was very important to keep one's eyes fixed on Jesus in order to measure the motivation and value of one's actions. One needs a mark to help gauge personal performance.

> As the end of our profession is the kingdom of God but the immediate aim or goal, is purity of heart, without which no one can gain that end: fixing our gaze then steadily on this goal as if on a definite mark, let us direct our course as straight towards it as possible.[17]

The struggle to overcome faults and grow in virtue is so much easier if one keeps the prize constantly before one's eyes. Without understanding and appreciating the spiritual principles and making them one's own, a person will have all the weariness of the journey without ever reaching one's destination.[18]

Christ is at the centre of Cassian's teaching on prayer and spiritual knowledge.[19] According to his Christology, Jesus' earthly ministry was exemplary, providing a model for approaching God with a 'pure disposition of heart'.[20] Cassian's own words in his first conference, is a good summary of his Christology, 'when our gaze has wandered ever so little from [Christ] let us turn the eyes of the soul back to Him'.[21] Everything depends on this return of the heart and keeping one's gaze fixed on Jesus.

The 'Tower Metaphor': A Call in Prayer to Real Participation in the Glorified Christ

For Cassian, imitation of Christ is the way to recover the full image and likeness of God in the perfection of love.[22] He wants to encourage his readers to move beyond Jesus' instruction on prayer, or example of prayer in His earthly life, to real participation in the Glorified Christ. Cassian teaches that Jesus is 'the very fount of inviolable sanctity' and the follower of Jesus, aspires to be for that reason, one who keeps one's gaze fixed on Jesus to see: 'the Glory of His Face and the image of his Splendour'.[23] Before addressing the teaching it is important to state that Cassian is not slow to acknowledge 'that we cannot possibly perform anything connected with the attainment of perfect virtue without [God's] assistance and Grace'.[24] In the light of this, one can only be puzzled as to how critics of his age and in later centuries accused him of deviating from the Gospel of Jesus or the teaching of the Church on Grace.[25]

In the Gospel 'tower metaphor', Cassian offers the would-be disciple three areas for consideration in embarking on the spiritual journey. Firstly there is a need for a firm *foundation*, in a life of renunciation and humility, by establishing oneself in absolute trust and dependence on God.[26] Secondly, there is a call to build up the *walls of virtue*, especially love through the *purging*[27] of faults and control of the passions. Finally there is the gift experience of prayer that crowns and completes the edifice, imaged in the uppermost cone of the tower.[28] Cassian takes great care to point out the reciprocal nature of these three levels in the transforming experience of prayer. The walls of virtue are purposeless without the cone experience of prayer communion with God. On the other hand he shows, that prayer intimacy with God is impossible without the prerequisite of a virtuous lifestyle, especially love of one's neighbour.[29] He then clarifies how the stability of both depends entirely on the foundation of absolute trust and faith dependency on God.[30] This foundation will be the subject of the forthcoming chapter.

Humility … is the mother of all virtues and the surest foundation of the whole spiritual superstructure. (*Conf*. 19.2)

Chapter One

The Foundation for the Spiritual Journey

Stability for the Spiritual Journey: 'Repent' in Humility

Cassian's first book, *Institutes*, deals specifically with the active life, which we might call today an apostolic life of good works. These institutes spell out basic modes of ethical behaviour expected of one who seriously considers following the Way of Our Lord, Jesus Christ. Cassian concludes this work with a concise descriptive introduction to his spirituality of the tower. He writes:

> Wherefore if we wish the summit of our building to be perfect and to rise well pleasing to God we should endeavour to lay its foundations according to the rules of evangelical strictness: which can only be the fear of God and humility, proceeding from kindness and simplicity of heart. But humility cannot possibly be acquired without giving up everything.[1]

In this presentation of the tower as a metaphor for the spiritual journey,[2] Cassian has Jesus' tower image in mind, and his teaching makes a strong parallel with the Gospel exhortation of Jesus especially in the final sentence.

> And indeed, which of you here, intending to build a tower, would not first sit down and work out the cost to see if one had enough to complete it? So in the same way, none of you can be my disciple unless you give up all your possessions (Lk 14:33).

Cassian uses a number of metaphors to image the spiritual journey. It is in his famous 'Treatise on Prayer' that he makes application of the tower image in a superb way.[3] He begins by establishing his teaching in the context of this teaching of Jesus:

> The parable of the gospel (Lk 14:28–33) teaches, whatever concerns the building of that spiritual and most lofty tower, is reckoned up and carefully considered beforehand … These things when prepared will be of no use nor allow the lofty height of perfection to be properly placed upon them, unless a clearance of all faults be first undertaken … and the strong foundations of simplicity and humility be laid … on that rock of the gospel (Lk 6:48) and by being built in this way this tower of spiritual virtues will … stand unmoved, and be raised to the utmost heights of heaven in full assurance of its stability.[4]

Humility: Central to the Foundation of Prayer

Cassian situates humility as central to the foundation of the spiritual journey. 'It is the mother of all virtues and the surest foundation of the whole spiritual superstructure.'[5] Hence it is the surest way toward acquiring purity of heart, which is fundamental to how it is acquired, persevered in, and crowned with the gift of contemplative prayer. In drawing attention to the Lord's teaching, 'Learn from me for I am gentle and humble of heart' (Mt 11:29), Cassian concludes that 'Humility … is the mistress of all virtues, it is the surest foundation of the heavenly building: it is the special and splendid gift of the Saviour.'[6] This is not the false humility, where one behaves and accepts treatment as a doormat and becomes an enabler to destructive behaviour. It is the realisation of where one's true identity lies, namely as 'the Beloved of God' and in this awareness, has understanding and compassion on the human condition, the limitations, faults and weaknesses in oneself and others, placing one's trust and dependence in God's abiding presence.

For the Desert Mothers and Fathers a word very closely linked to purity of heart and therefore to humility was *apatheia*. This Greek word meaning 'passionlessness' came to be used by them to mean freedom and detachment from desire and the passions. This state was understood as one of selfless love, harmony and peace. Cassian avoided using *apatheia*, as the term was prone to controversial misunderstanding. Instead, he used *puritas cordis* 'purity of heart' which indicates personal integration, the single-mindedness in readiness for contemplation and contemplative living.[7]

He defines purity of heart as 'purity and tranquillity of mind' and uses 'mind' synonymously with 'heart'. Tranquillity is the principal manifestation of purity of heart and often functions in place of it, as do similar concepts like stability and steadfastness.[8] He explains his teaching on purity of heart within the context of St Paul's presentation on love as the highest gift. Paul states, 'Though I should give away all that I possess, to the poor, and even give up my body to be burned – but if I am without love, it will do me no good whatsoever' (1 Co 13:3). Commenting on this he states:

> Perfection is not arrived at simply by self-denial, and the giving up of all our goods, and the casting away of honours, unless there is that charity, the details of which the Apostle describes, which consists in purity of heart alone.[9]

Keeping the focus on 'humility' as synonymous with 'purity of heart', and an essential requirement for the foundation of the spiritual edifice, the consideration now is on how it is acquired. The teaching begins with the rigour of practical experience for an enquiring disciple, before setting out on this journey.[10] The sole reason behind this experience was to provide the necessary opportunity for one to consider carefully beforehand the seriousness of the request, and to reflect on the possible destructive and negative consequences for anyone, who embarks on the journey of discipleship without proper discernment.[11] Regarding the dynamic in the acquisition, perseverance, and fruitfulness of humility, Cassian brings to our attention that the 'Fear of the Lord' is the beginning of wisdom and of our salvation, which gives rise to true sorrow for sin. This awareness gives birth to genuine humility and a desire to renounce inordinate desires bringing to an end faults that weigh one down. He states:

> Through mortification of desires, all faults are rooted out and decay. By driving out faults, virtues shoot up and increase. By the budding of virtues purity of heart is gained. By purity of heart the perfection of apostolic love is acquired.[12]

'Fear of the Lord', an Old Testament term used frequently by Cassian, does not refer to emotional fear but to 'right relationship with God' which gives rise to filial love and trust.[13] Humility is anchored in the beginning of our salvation. It has particular application to the laying of the foundation of prayer and is also essential for perseverance on the spiritual journey as well as being a prerequisite for the crowning perfection of apostolic love.

Prayer is fundamentally a Relational Experience

It is in the *Conferences* that Cassian addresses fully the call and challenge of prayer for contemplative living. Here he metaphorically and succinctly describes the reciprocal nature of the three stage levels of the spiritual journey. His specific teaching on the tower is linked directly to Jesus' radical teaching,[14] and where he elucidates the teaching in a superb way. He explains:

> First there must be laid the secure foundations of a deep humility, which may be able to support a tower that shall reach the sky: and next the spiritual structure of the virtues must be built up upon them and thus [finally] it may by little and little to rise to the contemplation of God.[15]

The realisation of the kingdom and reign of God in the human heart is for Cassian the ultimate aim of spirituality. He points out that it is fundamentally a relational experience in the call to prayer. The most effective way to enter this relationship is through the cultivation of a humble and pure heart, in a conversion process of renunciation, which begins in compunction. A closer study of this conversion process of compunction, and renunciation in fear of the Lord, will help to deepen the understanding in this foundation of deep humility.[16]

In Cassian's writings compunction means repentance or sorrow for sin. His study of compunction shows that tears are the most common form of spiritual experience, encompassing both keen sorrow and deep joy.[17] He exhorts a would-be disciple of Jesus to understand the awesomeness of the life which he is endeavouring to undertake, as a putting on: through God's grace the character, quality and mind of Christ in total self-emptying love.[18] Repentance today is understood as an experience of conversion, and in the sense that Keating describes: 'Repent' as a call 'to change the direction in which one is looking for happiness'[19] which will be considered in the final chapter.

The Primacy of Love in the Process of Conversion

Cassian clarifies and develops his teaching on renunciation by offering close up scriptural studies to illustrate how a humble and pure heart is acquired through an ever deepening threefold process of renunciation.[20] A particularly good example which he develops is God's call to Abraham, our father in Faith: 'Leave your country, your kindred, and your Father's house' (Gn 12:1). In the first call, 'Leave your country', Cassian sees an invitation to renounce all external things and possession of all riches in this world. In the second call, 'Leave your kindred', he exhorts one to renounce faults and practices from one's former way of life, which one is tied to from birth.[21]

'Leave your Father's house', Cassian interprets this third challenge as God's call to the soul to draw the mind away from visible things, renouncing every attachment and surrender to God in self-emptying love.[22] This threefold renunciation leads to complete detachment in body, mind and spirit after the example of our crucified Lord.[23] The final renunciation of every attachment in humility is the most important, and is in fact essentially the work of God. It is His free gift inviting the soul to a new and higher state of being in love. In fact unless this is reached, the first two renunciations are of little value on their own, though essential if the final one is to be attained. One can recognise here the origin of the purgative, illuminative and unitive stages of the spiritual journey as they were developed over the centuries. Cassian's teaching is extremely detailed, and he does not apologise for repeating the teaching from Scripture to highlight the importance of humility and purity of heart. The heart must be purified of all negative movements, of the false self, as a necessary prerequisite in readiness for the Lord to transform it into the resplendent beauty of His own image and likeness.[24]

Fear of the Lord which gives rise to genuine conversion, and inspires the soul to pursue the perfection of love, through this threefold renunciation, and flowers in a pure and humble heart, the immediate aim of the spiritual life. The Lord can then transform it into one of resplendent beauty, for a totally new way of loving, and being in the world. It is not only when the foundation of a humble heart is established, but also when one's lifestyle is transformed through the building up of the virtues, that a person is enabled to hear and respond to the Lord's loving invitation: 'Come into the land that I will show thee' (Gn 12:1).[25] This is the land of God's kingdom, the ultimate goal of prayer in the spiritual journey, and the crown of the 'heavenly building'.[26] This journey in transformation is the subject of the next chapter.

First there must be laid the secure foundations of a deep humility, which may be able to support a tower that shall reach the sky: and next the spiritual structure of the virtues must be built up upon them. (*Conf.* 9.3)

Chapter Two

The Spiritual Structure of the Virtues

Building up the Walls of Virtue – in 'Conversion' of Lifestyle
Keeping the imagery of the tower icon as the special focus of analyses for the spiritual journey, we now come to look at the building up of the walls of virtue on the firm foundation of simplicity and humility. To ensure that these walls of virtue are of endurable Gospel quality (Lk 6:48) serious work has to be brought to bear on addictive, destructive behaviour and passions. Only as these are controlled, or cut and dug out can the virtues grow and flourish.[1] The foundational preparations will be of no use 'unless a clearance of all faults be first undertaken' only in this way can the 'tower of spiritual virtues ... stand unmoved, and be raised to the utmost heights of heaven'.[2]

In colourful imagery, Cassian compares the nature of the soul to 'a fine feather', which if not damaged or spoilt, will rise naturally to the heights of heaven. In the same way the soul, if it is not weighed down or damaged by faults, will be raised by its own purity, to the heights.[3] He exhorts, 'By driving out faults, virtues shoot up and increase. By the budding of virtues, purity of heart is gained. By purity of heart, the perfection of apostolic love is acquired.'[4]

The Practical Challenge for Transformation of Heart

In terms of those things which concern the building of that spiritual and most sublime tower, attention to the passions and vices have to be carefully considered.[5] Like his contemporaries, Cassian uses the framework of the eight vices with their parallel virtues to present his ascetical teaching on how to enter the practical challenge of conversion, in order to bring about transformation of the heart: the proximate aim of the spiritual life. At first glance Cassian's presentation seems ruthless. But within the context of his whole teaching, it can only be understood as positive, necessary conditioning for the realisation of the ultimate goal, of the spiritual journey.

Cassian knew that whatever helps towards purity of heart, one must follow with all one's might, but whatever hinders one from it must be shunned as dangerous and hurtful.[6] The practical challenge in preparation for the crowning gift of prayer, calls for 'clearing away faults, laying a foundation of simplicity and humility, [and] building a spiritual tower of virtues raised to heaven'.[7] The eight principle faults or temptations which attack humankind, preventing spiritual growth, are: gluttony, fornication, avarice, anger, dejection, *acedia* (apathy), vainglory and pride.[8]

> They are basic tendencies toward evil, dangerous sources of sin, and habits of vice. The list suggests a complex of emotions, attitudes, desires and ways of acting which pervert good, useful impulses and which stand in the way of love for God, self, and others.[9]

The inordinate aspect of the temptation is a key consideration here and applies to all the vices as it leads to the abuse of good or natural impulses. What is necessary is always permitted, but any indulgence beyond that, is to be strictly disciplined or avoided.[10] This is the approach Cassian takes, and he presents two main groups within this eightfold framework. He pairs the first group as follows: gluttony and fornication, avarice and anger, dejection and *acedia*. Pride and vainglory, which belong to the second category and are related directly to the heart's movements, can play havoc in a soul.[11]

External Faults and their Remedies

In the first group the paired vices – namely gluttony with fornication, and avarice with anger – are linked together, in a relational, chain-like way, in such a manner that by giving into gluttony one is weakened in the more difficult combats. For from superfluity of gluttony, fornication is sure to spring, and from fornication covetousness, from covetousness anger, from anger, comes the internal fault of dejection, and from dejection, *acedia* (apathy).[12]

The temptation to gluttony, the inordinate use of food, is the first struggle. It is the easiest, but failure here rules one out of the contest. No control in this area leaves one more defenceless and vulnerable for more challenging temptations. For it is impossible, he maintained, 'for a full belly to make trial of the combat of the inner man, nor is he worthy to be tried in harder battles: who can be overcome in a slight skirmish'.[13]

Avarice and anger with gluttony and fornication are considered to be external faults because they are evoked by some form of external conditioning. Cassian describes avarice or covetousness 'as love of money'.[14] One must not only guard against the possession of money but also expel from our souls the desire for it, for example, cut off by the roots all dispositions towards it.[15]

Linked to avarice is anger, which 'rages within', or 'breaks out in word and deed and action' and can 'last for days'.[16] Like its paired counterpart avarice one ought not only banish anger from our actions but entirely root it out from our inmost soul,[17] because it is the greatest obstacle to prayer. Cassian continually connects the relevance of his teaching to the tower metaphor: If we are disturbed when attacked by anyone, it is clear that the foundations of humility have not been securely laid in us, and therefore at the outbreak even of a small storm, our whole edifice is shaken and ruinously disturbed.[18]

The remedies for conversion to be applied here: facilitate with the help of God the ground work for the building up of the walls of virtue. All of Cassian's teachings are grounded in the Scriptures and he quotes them continuously to uphold his stance: 'That is why you must kill everything in you that is earthly: sexual vice, impurity, uncontrolled passion, evil desires and especially greed, which is the same thing as worshipping a false god' (Col 3:5).[19]

Then, 'the diligent meditation on Scripture'[20] and watchfulness, in withdrawal from any material or thought that might feed temptation, ought to be adhered to. It is by living the Word, that discretion and right judgement are attained. This awakening leads one to an important insight which firmly anchors the cornerstone of 'purity of heart' in position for the 'whole spiritual superstructure'.[21] Hence our peace of mind lies in our own control, and so the fact that we are not angry ought not to result from another's perfection but from our own virtue, which is acquired not by someone else's patience but by our own long suffering.[22]

Cassian continually reminds his readers that every effort towards accomplishing one's purpose is indebted to God's grace, as Stewart points out: 'To place confidence in ascetical discipline alone without acknowledging the need for grace can forfeit whatever progress has been made.'[23] When these four obstructive hindrances are identified and disciplined in the practice of virtue, with the cornerstone of purity of heart, well positioned, then the building can proceed with God's grace.

Internal Faults and their Remedies

In addressing the internal faults Cassian describes the spirit of dejection as 'that [which] keeps one, back from all insight into Divine Contemplation … It makes one impatient and rough in all duties of work and devotion … It crushes and overwhelms the feelings with penal despair.[24] He describes *acedia* (apathy) as a lack of commitment to spiritual values, to carelessness, listlessness, and unconcern. The ancient texts have been re-examined from a psychiatric viewpoint as indicative of a form of depression: it is a chronic state of inability to be committed to a way of life or to a community.[25]

To be attacked by *acedia* is to be in a most wretched state.[26] Persons inflicted by this would have begun to progress steadily in the building up of the 'spiritual edifice'. However in the effort of the building, they lose sight of the 'cornerstone purity of heart without which no one, can gain the end',[27] namely the kingdom of God, 'the crown of the building of all the virtues'.[28] Cassian exposes this malady as 'weariness or distress of heart'.[29] It makes one lazy and sluggish about all manner of work which has to be done;[30] it makes one idle and lazy, without making any spiritual progress, or it drives one out restless and indolent in the matter of all kinds of work.[31]

The wretched soul who is afflicted by this disease seeks solace for his weariness in 'slumber or flight'.[32] *Acedia* attacks the unsuspecting one, who is apparently making progress in the building of the spiritual edifice. It could indicate midway on the spiritual venture. The monotony of tedious routine strikes when one has lost sight of the goal, or comes to realise that the goal was never visualised in the first place. It is then that *acedia* attacks the unhappy soul like a 'strong battering ram', which if not confronted and overthrown will little by little lead one to abandon the challenge.[33]

This is where the warning and application of Jesus teaching (Lk 14:28–33), adhered to so faithfully by Cassian, demonstrates its urgency and relevance as the most effective means of preventing or remedying this situation. 'Whatever concerns the building of that spiritual and most lofty tower',[34] must be reckoned up and considered carefully, because no one can come to the contemplation of God 'without giving up all one's possessions' (Lk 14:33). This does not just refer to material possessions but to all attachments to the 'false self' in which one can be enslaved or imprisoned, and will be developed more fully in the final chapter. To be overcome by *acedia* is to be overcome by all the preceding faults or addictions.

In order to overthrow it, one has to strike at the root. One has to trace the disease backwards to the cause and apply the remedy from there.[35] Cassian draws here on a text of Paul. 'That you take pains to be quiet … Do your own business … Work with your own hands.'[36] He sees these virtues as 'healing medicines' for this affliction of *acedia*.[37] He develops the dynamic carefully, taking pains to show that one who fails to live these out is in grave danger of being gradually entangled by the chain of opposing vices, which culminate in *acedia*, the disorderly behaviour of ill-found leisure of idleness.[38]

The two virtues which Cassian lays particular emphasis on are 'to be quiet' and 'to work'.[39] He demonstrates in detail, that a person who is not faithful in living by these twin virtues, of quiet recollection and diligence in attending to one's work, is gradually overcome by either of the two extremes, of idle laziness – leading to weariness of heart, or a dissipated restlessness that propels one out … to meddle aimlessly in another's affairs.[40] Cassian exhorts that the only way one can overcome this double assault is to resist the extremes of 'sleep' or 'flight'. For this crucial stage Cassian summarises his extensive teaching with one saving remedy, namely 'to work'.[41] This work refers not only to manual work but would include Cassian's understanding of the essential work of pondering on the text of Scripture, for anyone seeking to follow Christ.

Left untreated, 'this deadly wound' of *acedia* leaves one floundering in a world of disillusionment, But when it is honestly confronted, resisted and overthrown, the one is on the way towards realising one's destiny, 'the extreme summit of perfection'.[42] Cassian keeps this powerful image of the tower constantly before the reader's mind, as a simple fundamental truth namely: that humility, 'purity of heart' as the foundation of all the virtues, on which our relationship with Christ is built cannot possibly be sustained without giving up everything in relation to the 'false self'.[43]

The Final Obstacle is Most Difficult to Eradicate

Vainglory and pride are the two final obstacles to be overthrown in the building endeavour of the 'spiritual edifice'. They are the most savage and difficult to eradicate. They belong to the second category of faults. Like the former group they are linked in a chainlike way, but their mode of attack is just the opposite.[44] 'They are actually aroused in an entirely different way and manner … For when the others are eradicated these latter if not checked flourish more vigorously.'[45]

Vainglory attacks every aspect of one's behaviour, prayer and spiritual life, and wrecks one's life with elusive blows. It brings 'ample destruction on the soul … simply by its assent and wish to gain praise and glory from others'.[46] Pride that is wholly spiritual 'is the most destructive of all virtues and robs and despoils a person of all righteousness and holiness … which like some pestilential disease attacks the whole person … like some brutal tyrant'.[47] Cassian describes it as 'trusting in the power of one's own will'[48] which led to the fall of our first parents and so it is with the ones who endeavour to achieve perfection by their own efforts alone. Cassian here warns: 'To place confidence in ascetical discipline alone without acknowledging the need for grace can forfeit whatever progress has been made.'[49]

The remedy here for vainglory is first of all 'prudent discretion',[50] and which Cassian describes as 'the mother of all the virtues',[51] a name which he also gives to humility, indicating that they are synonymous. Relying on Scripture for his teaching: 'If your eye, the lamp of your body is diseased, your whole body will be in darkness' (Mt 6:22–3).[52] It is only through clarity of vision that one discerns the futility of one's behaviour and shuns 'all vanity and boasting', refrains from seeking the favour of others and carry out his endeavours for God's sake alone.[53]

The remedy of pride is in its healing opposite, namely humility. It is the one virtue that Jesus asks his disciples to learn from Him. 'Learn from me, for I am gentle and humble in heart and you will find rest for your souls' (Mt 11:29). This is the virtue that establishes one in right relationship with God, others, oneself and all one's endeavours. Humility entails a surrender of one's self to God in a loving relationship of faith-filled trust.

> No structure of virtue can possibly be raised in our soul unless first the foundations of true humility are laid in our heart, which being securely laid may be able to bear the weight of perfection and love.[54]

Cassian repeats his teaching: humility cannot possibly be acquired without giving up everything, and as long as one is a stranger to this, it is impossible to 'attain the perfection of love'.[55] This is the integrity and consistency of life which is central to Cassian's teaching, namely that we ought to strive to be before prayer what we want to be at prayer.[56] Here we encounter the mystery of reciprocal love and 'the inseparable bond' between purity of heart, the eradication of faults, and the practice of virtue in preparation for the experience of prayer which will be explored in the next chapter.

The crown of the building of all virtues is the perfection of prayer.
(*Conf.* 9.2)

Chapter Three

The Crown of Contemplative Prayer

The Reciprocal Bond between Lifestyle and Prayer – 'Believe'

The essential integration and unity, which is characteristic of an authentic journey in the human transformation for communion with God, is evident in every aspect of Cassian's teaching.[1] This is what Keating has observed and developed magnificently for the spiritual hunger of our modern times, which will be considered in the final chapter. He returns again and again to Cassian's teaching on prayer, as Cassian continually returns to the tower parable of Jesus to highlight and emphasise this integration. This is the profound insight and the lynchpin of Cassian's teaching. Dr David Walker presents a very readable translation here on the beginning of Cassian's treatise on the crowning cone of prayer:

> The perfection of heart consists in an unceasing and uninterrupted perseverance in prayer ... and practise of every physical and spiritual effort. *There is between these two a reciprocal and inseparable bond.* For just as the edifice of all the virtues point to the perfection of prayer as its crown, so unless all things have been brought together and joined by this crown, it cannot in any way stand firm and stable.[2] [Emphasis added]

As with building a tower: acquiring 'perfection of heart for continual and unbroken perseverance in prayer' is a gradual interrelated process. Sustaining purity of heart, purging earthly faults for the growth of virtue, cannot be separated. In reality they cannot be distinguished. They are unified aspects of a single endeavour to attain the vision of God. Stewart observes that the biblical anchor for Cassian's doctrine of purity of heart is 'Blessed are the pure in heart, for they shall see God' (Mt 5:8). By linking purity of heart to the vision of God, this beatitude can connect the 'goal' to the 'end'.[3] In metaphorical language the foundation to the crown and all the structure in between, is built up little by little 'to rise to the contemplation of God'.[4]

Perseverance becomes a virtue to constantly befriend one in the vital task of acquiring 'an immovable tranquillity of mind and a perpetual purity', and of integrating all one's endeavours, as Cassian explains: 'Lasting and continual calmness in prayer ... cannot be secured ... without these virtues, so neither can, those virtues which lay its foundations be fully gained without persistence in it.'[5] With perseverance, which can be compared to a 'bonding agency', there can be no discrepancy between foundational purity of heart in an attitude of love, a virtuous lifestyle and communion with God. 'The threefold aspects of the ascent to God are actually concomitant, not consecutive.'[6] This is the ideal which Cassian holds out to his readers. 'Wherefore what we want to find ourselves like while we are praying, that we ought to prepare ourselves to be before the time for prayer.'[7] It is only in this way, Cassian teaches, that one can fulfil the exhortations of Scripture to 'pray constantly' (1 Th 5:17). He points out that 'we shall not be able to carry out that charge unless our minds, purified from all stains of sin, and given over to virtue as to its natural good, feed on the continual contemplation of Almighty God.'[8]

As the height of all perfection, consists in the consummation of prayer, it is not surprising that Cassian excels himself in expounding the character of this prayer and then how one can practise it without ceasing. Prayer is a unique experience and Cassian acknowledges that there are as many ways of praying as there are people.[9] This being said, he points out from Scripture the fourfold nature of vocal prayer 'I urge then, first of all, that petitions, prayers, intercessions and thanksgiving should be offered' (1 Tm 2:1).

Cassian expounds on each of these kinds of prayer and how they can be expressions of the 'most fervent and ardent prayers'. He concludes that: the first seems to belong more especially to beginners, who are still troubled by the recollection of their sins; the second to those who have already attained some loftiness of mind in their spiritual progress; the third to those who are so stimulated to intercede for others and also through the earnestness of their love; and the fourth being now free from care can contemplate with a pure mind, the beneficence of God.[10]

Cassian acknowledges that these four kinds of prayer can be the occasion of fervent and ardent prayer. This is especially true regarding the different types of application exemplified in the prayers of Jesus.[11] However, as Stewart points out, Cassian urges his readers to advance from prayer suitable to beginners,[12] 'of eliminating faults and cultivating virtues, to the prayer of contemplation, arising from the fervour of love'.[13]

The Role of Scripture:
in leading to full Christian Maturity

In terms of Cassian's 'tower that shall reach the sky',[14] metaphorically speaking, we are now approaching the prayer of the 'extreme summit of perfection'.[15] Before exploring this 'crown of the building',[16] a word must be said in Cassian's pedagogy, about the role of Scripture, for raising one to the full stature of Christian maturity. The primary source for Cassian's teaching is the Bible.[17] His love and knowledge of Scripture is evident on every page of his writing, where he quotes the Scriptures freely to support his teaching. Cassian developed a framework for a Scripture approach to prayer which later became known as *lectio divina.*

> *Lectio divina* refers to a holy reading of the Scriptures ... It is thus distinguished from scientific exegesis, hermeneutics, and the study of Scripture for specifically theological purposes ... The desired result of application to *lectio divina* is a thorough assimilation of sacred truth and a life lived according to this truth.[18]

According to Stewart this is 'Cassian's greatest influence on the Latin tradition'.[19] He recommended the reflective pondering on the text of Scripture known as *meditatio* as an essential work for anyone seeking to follow Christ, and especially as a remedy for combating faults and fostering virtue.[20] Commenting on this, Stewart writes:

> More important than physical disciplines are the spiritual ones of *reading*, *meditatio*, and *unceasing prayer*. The practices of *meditatio* of the scriptures and unceasing prayer constitute the hinge between the ascetical and contemplative aspects of human life, filling the mind and heart with good material

> while blocking the intrusion of destructive thoughts.[21] [Emphasis added]

Following *meditatio* and closely associated with it, was *oratio*, meaning 'when the heart spoke from its appropriation of the text'. For Cassian, *lectio*, reading; *meditatio* – reflecting, and *oratio* – responding in prayer, though not identical, were inseparable.[22] This framework for praying the Scriptures has enriched Western monastic prayer up to the present day. 'Contemporary attention to *lectio divina* beyond monastic circles concerns the importance of an informed yet spiritual interpretation of and reflection on Sacred Scripture by all the baptised.'[23] The final stage of *lectio* is contemplation; namely resting in the presence of God. It is here that Cassian excels himself as a teacher of prayer and an authority today on the spiritual journey.

The spiritual journey for Cassian entails a resolute commitment to the process, 'little by little'.[24] The imagery here in relation to the tower is that of persevering steadily 'block by block' towards the uppermost heights of the most lofty tower.[25] In this way the faithful disciples prepare their heart for God's gift of a still more lofty form of prayer, namely the Lord's Prayer. In this prayer Cassian teaches that a still more sublime and exalted stage is brought about: by the contemplation of God alone, in fervent love, by which the mind, transporting and flinging itself into love for Him, addresses God most familiarly as its own Father.[26] In making this confession, we acknowledge our liberation from the slavery of sin and our adoption as God's children.[27]

With regard to Cassian's teaching on the Lord's Prayer, Stewart makes the following observation. Cassian interprets its opening words to be about passing through earthly life as safely and speedily as possible in order to reach the heavenly reality, signified by calling God 'Father'.[28] He goes through each petition, showing how they manifest God's reign in the heart of one, whose petitions are focused only on the eternal,[29] and made in humility, charity and tranquillity of heart.[30]

The Most Sublime Form of Prayer

This teaching is explored more fully in Cassian's most developed description of contemplative prayer, 'when God shall be all our love'[31] and we are joined to Him by a lasting and inseparable affection. Having unfolded the importance of the Lord's Prayer for his readers Cassian introduces the most sublime form of prayer, apex of his teaching and crown of 'the whole spiritual superstructure'.[32] Dr David Walker again gives us a very readable translation on this important teaching. This most sublime prayer 'which is truly ineffable' raises those who make it their own to that more exalted state:

> It transcends all human sense and is not characterised by any sound of the voice, or movement of the tongue, or any pronunciation of words. The mind illumined by that infusion of heavenly light, does not describe it in human or limited language, but … ineffably utters it to God, producing such things in that brief moment of time, that returned to itself, it cannot easily speak about them.[33]

Jesus himself is our model for this form of prayer, which 'when He retired alone in the mountain He is said to have poured forth in silence'.[34] Because this sublime prayer of silence in contemplation transcends nature, it is not easy to describe or explain. It can be experienced as 'inexpressible delight', 'salutary conviction', 'incontrollable joy', or 'in complete silence within the secrets of a profound quiet, the delight of the heart'.[35]

In this prayer as in all true prayer, faith is the indispensable requirement for it to be efficacious.[36] To support this, Cassian quotes St Mark, 'I tell you therefore, everything you ask and pray for, believe that you have it already, and it will be yours' (Mk 11:24). This quote resonates with Jesus' words, 'In truth I tell you, in no one in Israel have I found faith as great as this' (Mt 8:10). It is this faith, *pistis*[37] that is at the heart and summit of Cassian's tower metaphor for the spiritual journey. The biblical commentary on this verse states that:

> The faith that Jesus asks for from the outset of his public life (Mk 1:15) and throughout his subsequent career, is that act of trust and self-abandonment by which people no longer rely on their own strength and policies but commit themselves to the power and guiding word of him in whom they believe.[38]

'Faith demands the sacrifice of the whole person, mind and heart.'[39] It is in the context of this faith response that Jesus explains, 'None of you can be my disciple unless you give up all your possessions' (Lk 14:33). It is this faith that enables one to enter the 'crowning cone' of transcendent prayer. It is this leap of faith in trustful love and confidence in God that conditions one to receive the gift to pray 'not for our own advantage or for temporal comforts but in conformity with the Lord's will'.[40]

The Prayer of Complete Silence

Willingness to surrender all to God in trust and faith-filled love conditions a person to receive the outpouring of God's love (Jn 14:23). The 'ardent and ineffable prayer' which transcends all thoughts, words, and language, is the prayer of complete silence and exemplified by Jesus in his prayer alone to the Father,[41] and in his teaching on prayer: 'When you pray, go to your private room, and when you have shut the door, pray to your Father who is in that secret place, and your Father who sees all that is done in secret will reward you' (Mt 6:6).

It is to this intimacy with the Father that the faith-filled disciple is invited. Cassian expounds Jesus' teaching as follows:

> This is how we can achieve this. We pray within our room, when we remove our heart completely from the din of all thoughts and anxieties, and in some secret and intimate way, we disclose our prayers to the Lord. We pray with closed doors, when with sealed lips and in deep silence we pray, not to the searcher of words, but the searcher of hearts. We pray in secret when with fervent heart and mind we lay open our petitions to God alone.[42]

According to Stewart 'Cassian suggests that Jesus' own prayer in solitude was of the silent and ecstatic kind which Cassian describes as the highest form of prayer.'[43] This is the exalted state that 'truly ineffable flame prayer' to which the fervent praying of the Lord's Prayer leads one. This state of transcendent prayer is the fruit of the well-tilled earth of the heart.[44] 'As one progresses, Christ becomes the object of contemplation, rather than the teacher of prayer, drawing one into the very centre of "indissoluble love"[45] between Father and Son.'[46] This is the 'crowning cone' of the tower and 'the pinnacle of the spiritual life'.[47] Cassian exercising his 'great charisma as a teacher'[48] gently guides the labouring souls who long to see Jesus to rise with Him from low and earthly works and thoughts and go apart in the lofty mountain of solitude which is free from the disturbance of all earthly thoughts and troubles, and secure from the interference of all sins, and being exalted by pure faith and the heights of virtue reveals the glory of His Face and the image of His splendour to those who are able to look on Him with pure eyes of the soul.[49]

Cassian interprets this rising with Jesus as perfect bliss and the fulfilment of 'that prayer of the Saviour'.[50] 'May they all be one: Father, may they be one in us, as you are in me and I am in You' (Jn 17:21). This experience of intimacy with God is arrived at gradually 'little by little' and 'step by step', until God becomes:

> All our love, and every desire, and wish and effort, every thought of ours and all our life and words and breath and that unity which already exists between the Father and the Son, and the Son and the Father, has been shed abroad in our hearts and minds, so that as He loves us with a pure and unfeigned and indissoluble love, so we may be joined to Him by a lasting and inseparable affection.[51]

To the very end Cassian keeps focusing the reader's attention on the sublime tower as a most apt teaching aid for this journey in prayer. In order to reach 'this inmost shrine and lofty heights of perfection'[52] the foundations 'must first be firmly laid and afterwards the towering heights of perfection ... can be placed and raised upon them'.[53] What has now to be addressed and learned regarding this lofty state of prayer, is, 'the power by which continuance in it might be gained and kept'.[54]

Continual Awareness of the Presence of God

In Cassian's perception, to enquire on how to realise continual awareness of the presence of God, is a clear indication of one's readiness for this form of prayer.[55] Before disclosing the method for engaging in unceasing prayer, he reminds his readers again of the other essential prerequisites. These are a sustained endeavour to live a virtuous lifestyle on the sure foundation of humility and purity of heart. Without these, an 'unbroken continuance in prayer'[56] is impossible. The sacred formula handed down 'by the oldest fathers',[57] 'which everyone in his progress towards continual awareness of God, is invited to ponder and turn over ceaselessly in [their] heart is'; 'O God come to my assistance: O Lord make haste to help me' (Ps 70:1).[58] This verse Cassian explains has been carefully selected from the whole of the Scriptures for this purpose:

> It embraces all the feelings which human nature can experience, and it can be suitably and appropriately adapted to every situation and temptation. It contains an invocation to God against every danger; it includes the humility of a pious confession; it embraces that watchfulness which goes with zeal and continual fear; it contains awareness of one's weakness, trust in the response; and the assurance of God's ever-present and ever-ready help.[59]

Commenting on the teaching of this whole chapter, Chadwick states that it is 'one of the beautiful passages of all Christian writing during more than a thousand years of religious devotion'.[60] Although the 'Jesus prayer'[61] is perhaps the most famous, Cassian may well be the first to give full articulation to the continuous repetition of an evocative verse.[62] We have known this verse traditionally as the beginning of the various Hours of the Divine Office. However, it was originally intended as a way of coming to awareness of God, and a means of passing from pre-occupations with the things of the world to the experience with God. That is why it came to be placed at the beginning of the Hours.[63]

Cassian proceeds to demonstrate the efficacy of this prayer formula and how it can help one to engage in every aspect of one's journey in prayer, demonstrating again the interrelatedness of each stage, from the foundation to the cone of contemplative prayer. This prayer formula can be aptly applied to the onslaught of each temptation. It 'is an impregnable wall for all who are labouring under the attacks of demons, as well as an impenetrable coat of mail and a strong shield'.[64] This echoes so closely St Paul's exhortation and also St Patrick's for the spiritual combat: on the need to put on the full armour of God in the struggle against the ruling forces of darkness in this world.[65] Paul states:

> That is why you must rely on God's armour, or you will not be able to put up any resistance when the worst happens … So stand your ground, with truth buckled round your waist, and integrity for a breastplate, wearing for shoes on your feet the eagerness to spread the Gospel of peace and always

> carrying the shield of faith so that you can use it to put out the burning arrows of the evil one. And then you must accept salvation from God to be your helmet, and receive the Word of God from the Spirit to use as a sword (Ep 6:13–17).

Paul goes on to exhort the early Christians 'to keep praying in the Spirit on every possible occasion' (Ep 6:18). Cassian teaches how this can be done. This verse which contains the glow of love and charity 'will be found helpful and useful to every one of us in whatever condition we may be … not only in sorrowful and hard matters but also equally in prosperous and happy ones'.[66] It is to be prayed also when the soul experiences 'the visitation of the Holy Spirit' and gains 'purpose of soul, steadfastness of thought, keenness of heart, together with ineffable joy and transport of mind'.[67]

Just as the performance of an archer or athlete depends on the quantity and quality of the preceding practice, so Cassian exhorts the disciple, whose goal is 'perfect and sublime prayer', must endeavour to practise continual recollection of God through the use of this sacred formula. Therefore what we want to be at prayer, we should be before the time of prayer. The mind will be formed at the time of prayer by the state which preceded it.[68] Again to illustrate this, Cassian uses a very apt metaphor, in which he compares the image of a miller to the disciple, in this regard. He likens the heart to the millstone. It will grind whatever is fed into it. Like the miller, it is the disciple who decides on the quantity and quality of the input.[69] Hence the importance of praying this sacred formula on every possible occasion.

No one is Excluded from the Secret Chamber of God's Love

This is the prayer of one who becomes 'grandly poor' through the poverty of this single verse, to experience the bliss of the kingdom of heaven.[70] With persevering love and diligent care, Cassian gently guides those who long for communion with God towards the secret chamber of His Love (Mt 6:6) 'to that invisible and celestial contemplation'.[71] He takes pains to explain how this may come about:

> Strengthened by the constant use of it, and by continual meditation, it casts off and rejects the rich and full material of all manner of thoughts, and restricts itself to the poverty of this one verse, and so arrives with ready ease at that beatitude of the gospel, which holds the first place … 'Blessed are the poor in spirit: for theirs is the kingdom of heaven' (Mt 5:3).[72]

This prayer of the poor in spirit is characterised by not using any words or utterances. With the purpose of mind inflamed it arises through ecstasy of heart by 'some unaccountable keenness of spirit' and the mind, without the 'aid of the senses or any visual material pours it forth to God' with unutterable groaning and sighs that cannot be uttered.[73] The spirit too comes to help us in our weakness, for when we do not know how to pray properly, then the spirit personally makes our petitions for us in groans that cannot be put into words (Rm 8:26).

This is the 'ardent prayer' to which the 'Our Father' leads one beyond earthly concerns, into the intimacy of the Blessed Trinity. When this unity enjoyed by the Father and the Son has permeated the senses and mind through 'the visitation of the Holy Spirit',[74] then we are united with God 'in a lasting and inseparable affection'.[75] In this experience, the prayer of Jesus: 'Father … that they may be one as we are one, with me in them and you in me, may they be so completely one that the world will realise that it was you who sent me' (Jn 17:22–3) is fulfilled.[76]

For this 'highest learning' by which one is taught to 'cleave to God'[77] Cassian, with the aid of his tower metaphor reiterates his teaching that 'the foundations must first be firmly laid' then 'gradually step by step mount up' from the lowest depths to the 'towering heights of perfection' where one arrives 'without difficulty' at the inmost shrine and lofty heights of perfection.[78]

Extraordinary gift as this 'perfection of heart' is, Cassian insists that no one is excluded from receiving it, on account of rustic simplicity or an inability to read. 'The possession of purity of heart and mind lies close to all',[79] if only they will keep them fixed on God, through the meditation of this single verse in poverty of spirit. Then 'the Kingdom of heaven will be theirs' (Mt 5:3).[80]

Surely this has to be a way forward for genuine renewal in the Church predicted by the prophets of our day, as it has been in past centuries with certain adaptations to the prayer formula,[81] and can be identified here in this well-loved Irish hymn which was sung by all the people:

1. *Deus meus adiuva me (My God, help me).*
Tabhair dom do shearc, a Mhic ghil Dé, x 2
Give me love of Thee, O Son of God x 2
Deus meus adiuva me (My God, help me).

4. *Domine, Domine, exaudi me (Lord, Lord, hear me).*
M'anam bheith lán de d'ghrá, a Dhé, x 2
May my soul, O God, be full of love for Thee.
Domine, Domine, exaudi me (Lord, Lord, hear me).[82]

Show us some theme for reflection by which God can be conceived in the mind and continuously held … setting it before our eyes … we have something which we can look at. (*Conf.* 10.8)[1]

CHAPTER FOUR

The Irish Dimension

St Patrick carried the Teaching of Cassian to Ireland

Our consideration now is the Irish Dimension but only in relation to that which pertains to Cassian's teaching on the tower as a framework for the transforming experience of prayer. It has been historically established that Cassian's writings were widely read throughout Gaul,[2] as well as accompanying the Benedictine movement as it spread throughout Europe. In fact, 'Cassian dedicated his second set of *Conferences* to Honoratus, still superior of the enormous monastic community at Lérins.'[3] This was the renowned St Honoratus of Arles, bishop, founder and first abbot of this famous monastery in AD410, and who died in Arles in AD430.[4] The *Institutes* and *Conferences* dominated thought in Lérins and the surrounding hermitages,[5] where a solitary life was held in higher esteem than the communal monastic form of life.[6]

According to the seventh-century 'Life of Patrick' by Muirchú, Patrick (*c.*AD389–461) spent a considerable number of years in Gaul,[7] at the same time as Cassian.[8] It has been suggested by Liam de Paor, that Patrick may have spent some time at the monastery of Lérins.[9] This proposal is agreed by most, if not all Irish historians, and has been convincingly argued by John Ryan.[10] In the first half of the fifth century Lérins was the holy isle *par excellence* of Europe. Here Patrick studied and acquired that excellent knowledge of the Holy Scriptures and that solid grounding in Catholic teaching which stood him in good stead when he came to Ireland. 'The Irish System of Monasticism was remotely Egyptian, but hailed more proximately from Lérins, whence it came directly through St Patrick.'[11] Patrick could not lose so favourable an opportunity of acquiring spiritual training of unusual value. His life under the care of Honoratus would be just like that of other monks.[12]

> Patrick trained as a monk, loved the monastic order, but it was as a cleric, not a monk that he began his missionary work among the people of Ireland[13] 'with the island monastery as his objective'.[14] It was a well known desire of Patrick: 'that the land [would] abound with monks.[15]

In the early period of Irish Monasticism Cassian was the great teacher in matters pertaining to prayer. Patrick carried this spirit and teaching of Cassian in person to Ireland.[16] The strong influence of Cassian would also have come during the centuries that followed, with the journeying of monks as they spread the monastic movement[17] and by the circulation of his writings.[18] As well as the admonition of St Benedict (*c.*480–547) to his monks, to read Cassian: St Gregory the Great (*c.*540–604) and St Columbanus (*c.*543–615) were considered his successors and both also drew heavily on his teaching for *The Book of the Pastoral Rule* and *The Monastic Rule* respectively.[19] Ryan's classic work on early Irish Monasticism outlines almost in paraphrase Cassian's *Conferences* on prayer, as the major influence in this early period,[20] and which are directly related to the sublime tower metaphor. He states that:

> A very large proportion of Irish monks … were capable of unbroken contemplation. The evidence of this is the growth of the eremitical habit.[21] Though the body of Irish monasticism was predominantly monastic, the spirit which animated it was everywhere eremitical.[22]

The Beehive 'Clochán': A Prominent Feature of Early Irish Monasticism

At Lérins the highest honour was paid to the hermits rather than to the monks within the monastery. 'Cassian was here a respected teacher, and we may be sure that his doctrine on the interrelation between the eremitical and the monastic way of life was approved and put into practice.'[23] The theory of religious life, including his teaching on the sublime tower as a framework for one's journey in prayer, formulated so splendidly by Cassian was accepted in Ireland, and led directly to the hermitage, once the process of purification for the monk in the monastic life, was complete.[24]

The need to be well trained in the discipline of the monastic life was essential before one was ready to take on the challenge of a life in solitude. 'Just as contemplation was looked upon as the normal result of a spiritual life of self-conquest and prayer, so it was expected that some among the contemplatives would reach mystical heights in their union with God.'[25] There can be no doubt that the Irish monks regarded the solitary way of life as more perfect than the monastic way, hence the general tendency to seek out the 'desert'. Towards the end of the sixth century the preference for a life of solitude was so prominent a feature of religious life, that it marked the beginning of a new era.[26] The evidence of this is the increase in the number of anchorites who retired to a *clochán* – a beehive cell, as an abode for solitude.

This era in the ascetic tradition, which became a marked feature of Irish monasticism in the sixth century, remained particularly strong until the eighth century, when it suffered a temporary decline with the growth and secularisation of the great monastic centres. By the late eighth century a reaction to this state of affairs resulted in 'a great Irish ascetic and anchoritic revival'.[27] The reformers were determined to remove from the monastic ideal any preoccupation with secular affairs, and sought very persuasively, a return to the desert ideal of sublime prayer and asceticism.[28]

As has been pointed out, a particular characteristic of Irish monasticism was the desire to imitate as closely as possible the monastic pattern of the first desert monks of Egypt. In adhering to this spirit, these Irish monks of the renewal constantly sought the equivalent of the Egyptian desert. *The Antiphonary of Bangor,* written between 680 and 691, makes some nineteen references to Egypt; the attitude embodied in them is summed up perfectly in one of the quatrains:

> A House full of Delights;
> Built on Rock:
> A veritable vine:
> Transmitted from Egypt.[29]

A Valuable Link in the History of the Round Tower

G. L. Barrow quoting from Adamnán's splendid work on the Life of Columba[30] relates a short story on how the saint who died in 597 miraculously saved one of the brethren in a fall *de monasterii culmine rotunda*, meaning 'from the round summit of the monastery'. The dating of the building of the first towers here, much earlier than generally believed; is disputed or dismissed by modern scholars.[31] However reference to the term *monasterium* is highly significant in relation to this present consideration. G. L. Barrow concludes with Petrie and Reeves, both authorities in ancient architecture,[32] that:

> The story [is] 'a most valuable link in the history of round towers' since the use of the term *monasterium* instead of *cloig-theach* indicates that their primary use was as monastic abodes ... If correct this is the first record of any round tower.[33]

G. L. Barrow claims that the round tower is possibly 'an elongated *clochán*'.[34] I go further and agree with George Petrie who is more definite in his claim. He asserts that round towers were anchorite towers.[35] Monks favoured with the desire for 'mystical heights in their union with God'[36] could retire to a *clochán*, a beehive hut or cell to live unfettered, in communion with God. 'Cell' being the original meaning of *Kill*, a place name associated with so many monastic settlements throughout Ireland and an elongated *clochán* was central to the settlements which developed into monasteries to 'become new centres of Irish civilisation'.[37]

It was during this period of revival, that most of the round towers were built.[38] The Irish Monastic system lasted for almost seven centuries when it finally collapsed and gave way to an influx of new forms of religious life from abroad,[39] and the austere Rule of the Cistercians appealed to the Irish churchmen.[40] 'Here was a way of life with the physical austerity, spiritual devotion, and commitment of the Irish ascetics, together with the organisation which twelfth-century opinion recognized as necessary.'[41] It is the general opinion of historians that the building of the round towers ceased during this transition period.[42] It seems that it was at this time of renewal in the Church under St Malachy and the new orders of Cistercians and Augustinians that the existing round tower took on its better known name as a *cloig-theach*, a bell-tower.[43] In this way it provided not only a visual but also an audible call of prayer as the monastery expanded with a more structured lifestyle and 'the need to regulate the work, rest and prayer within the monastic community'.[44]

The Round Tower: A Visible Icon of Cassian's Teaching on the Call to Prayer

There has been considerable debate among scholars in recent centuries regarding the enigmatic mystery of the towers and regarding their origin and use.[45] In the nineteenth century Daniel O'Byrne concluded 'age after age obscurity has compassed the origin and use of the round towers' and he asks two very poignant questions. Namely, who were their founders? And for what purpose were they founded?[46] In the nineteenth century George Petrie declared that, 'the towers are of Christian and ecclesiastical origin and were erected at various periods between the fifth and thirteenth century' and as stated earlier that they were built originally as anchorite towers.[47]

In our own day, the award-winning architect Brian Lalor in his magnificent architectural research on the round tower still acknowledges the fascination which the round towers still hold today, despite the 'enigmatic feature' of their origin and purpose[48] and rightly deplores the lack of research in this area.[49] Roger Stalley has since published his research. He claims that the towers have a three-hundred-year span of building and he examines the pros and cons of their function as belfries[50] but concludes, 'the overall picture is thus extremely confused, and states that for the time being the origin of the Irish tower remains an open question'.[51] The proposition which I make here is: that the main objective for building the sublime round tower was first and foremost as a *visible icon* of Cassian's teaching on the foundation, lifestyle and ultimate goal of the monk or would-be disciple, and functioned concurrently or sequentially as an abode for solitude and channel for an audible bell call to prayer as taught by Cassian.

The Scriptures are the living Word of God for all time. Cassian's exposition of the parable of the tower (Lk 14:28–33) has significant relevance for all who today are embarking on the spiritual journey into the reign in God. Endeavours to apply his teaching will most surely contribute towards bringing to fulfilment a 'new civilisation of love' where justice and peace will be established for all.[52] I trust that what is presented here of Cassian's teaching on the tower as a icon for personal transformation through prayerful communion with God will cast new and challenging light on the obscurity regarding their origin and use. This challenge is further articulated by Dr Michael Ryan who states that the final question posed by Stalley's research is 'what do the towers symbolise in this new millennium'?[53] It is my hope that the final chapter of this work will be an attempt to address this timely question.

This Mystery … is Christ among you, your hope of Glory.
(Col 1:27)

CHAPTER FIVE

Contemporary Application of the Tower Metaphor

The Tower Metaphor: A Pedagogical Masterpiece for all Time

Cassian's sublime tower icon is a pedagogical masterpiece, in presenting a framework for the spiritual journey in prayer. It portrays powerfully the reciprocal dynamic in a person's human growth and transformation in a manner exemplified by Jesus, who identified Himself as the Way to the Father (Jn 14:7), and which He invites all humankind to follow. Jesus' use of 'Abba' when He turned to God was unique ... This word captures the mystery of Jesus' identity and mission: in a full filial relationship with God.[1]

The challenge to follow Christ (Lk 14:33) applied so aptly by Cassian, is the call to every human being to realise one's full personhood in an I-Thou faith-awakening experience in God (Ep 4:13). It is an invitation to mature as a full human person into a glorious destiny of communion in God's Trinitarian Love (Ep 1:4–6, 11–13), and which appears to be the particular hunger of this present time. It has certainly been once more a wake-up call for me personally.

This call is a call to contemplative living, 'to build up the Body of Christ', a clarion call promulgated magnificently in our own day, until we all reach unity in faith and knowledge of the Son of God and form the perfect New Humanity in Christ.[2] It is a call to a spirituality of communion earnestly expressed by Pope John Paul II, who takes care to point out the essential role of prayer in all pastoral endeavours in this regard.[3] The call is universal, but the faith-awakening experience is always personal, and the process of transformation is normally gradual. Speaking of this process His Holiness, Pope John Paul II stated: 'It is a question of gradually and patiently coming to know what lies deep within and of harmonising the various elements that make each of us unique, original and unrepeatable.'[4]

The three transformational stages of the spiritual journey in prayer, foundational purification, gradual illumination through conversion of lifestyle, and transformation in union with God are clearly defined, and aptly applied in Cassian's teaching. 'All the guides to spirituality in which Western Europe later abounded, were his descendants.'[5] With certain language, cultural or framework adaptations, these three stages are easily discernable in the lives and teaching of the mystics down to the present day, each in their own unique, original and unrepeatable manifestations.[6]

In considering the limitations and strengths of the tower metaphor some people may prefer or find 'journey' or 'centring' metaphors for the spiritual journey, more helpful than the 'ascent model' such as the tower. Each metaphor will have certain limitations in endeavouring to express the human encounter with 'the Mystery of Christ' (Ep 3:5). But in the measure that a metaphor succeeds in elucidating the meaning and reality it signifies, it achieves its purpose. The fact that Cassian was addressing monks could deter a person from considering the teaching, until one comes to realise that the call of the monk with regard to discipleship is the same for all humankind,[7] namely 'to be open to one's eternal potential in Christ',[8] albeit in different modes of expression, or vocation (Ep 3:5–9).

The particular strength of the tower icon is firstly that the teaching is based on the living Word of Scripture. When the symbolism is explained, its application can be powerful and profound (Heb 4:12), and it lends itself easily to explaining Jesus' teaching on radical discipleship throughout the Gospels.[9] An impressive example would be the opening words in Jesus' ministry, 'Repent [be converted][10] and believe in the Good News' (Mk 1:15). Repent, in laying the foundation in purity of heart and motivation. Then be converted, from a self-centred lifestyle of the false self, to a virtuous life in other-centred love of the true self, in readiness for the gift of believing, of faith-awakening communion in God's abiding presence. I have actually applied Cassian's teaching on the tower to this proclamation of Jesus, in individual and group situations, only to receive a joyous response in an expressed recognition, of a first-time comprehensive understanding of Jesus' message and meaning in terms of radical discipleship, and Eucharistic living.

Yearning Today for a Deeper Relationship with God

In our technological society there are many signs of fragmentation and alienation in the human person, where materialism and consumerism have become its new ethos. 'Ours is a new age of history with critical and swift upheaval spreading gradually to all corners of the earth.'[11] Inequalities and cut-throat competition have given rise to all kinds of corruption, exploitation and crime, resulting in various levels of mistrust, fear, alienation and loneliness, with many no longer able to discern life's meaning. The present situation echoes the fulfilment of the prophetic word, when there will be: A famine in the country, not of hunger for food, nor thirst for water, but for hearing the Word of God (Am 8:11).

The turbulence, confusion and famine experienced within the church and society in recent decades has given rise to a phenomenal interest in spirituality,[12] at grass-root levels of both Church and society,[13] with many yearning for a deeper personal relationship with God. We are at a turning point as described so comprehensively by Bede Griffiths.[14] It is at this turning point, that the excellence of Cassian's teaching on the sublime tower can have particular if not unique relevance.[15] It demonstrates for the individual, the importance of realising that there is an inseparable integration between the three stages of growth, in the transformative process of becoming 'a new creation in Christ' (2 Co 5:17).[16]

The universal call to holiness and the perfection of love has been once again proclaimed in our times[17] and needs to be heard more than ever today,[18] and with the phenomenal growth of interest in spirituality,[19] it is being heard. Books, audio tapes and websites available on the subject of spirituality, have multiplied at a remarkable rate since Vatican II. This is in response to the hunger for God's Word in a renewed and deeper search for life's meaning. The search has given rise to worldwide encouragement in bible-study initiatives,[20] as well as networks of contemplative and centring prayer. The Contemplative Outreach Movement[21] and the World Community of Christian Meditation,[22] are, according to Richard Rohr,[23] 'the best known and most systematic teaching of a Christian contemplative practice today'.[24]

New Findings and Insights in Modern Psychology

Here Thomas Keating is of noteworthy mention. He is a disciple of Cassian and bases his library of inspirational works on Cassian's teaching, with all the additional insights and findings of modern psychology.[25] He presents the teaching of Cassian in contemporary language to address the problems of our time. Keating acknowledges Cassian as a significant author of this method of prayer which culminates in the 'Pure Prayer'[26] of resting in God, and adapts the teaching in a method of centring prayer which is easy to follow and put into practice.[27]

The particular question for our time is this contemporary application of the tower metaphor. How can the people of this present age be awakened to the urgency of this living challenge for the future growth and wellbeing of humanity? It is on how the challenge and call to holiness can be addressed in today's confused and bewildered world, where Keating merits our attention. A founding member of the worldwide movement of Contemplative Outreach, he addresses this for us as an experienced teacher of 'the Way'. He draws our attention to how Cassian's teaching on prayer has been further developed by mystics down through the centuries, but lost to the mainstream church since the Reformation, and encouraged today, particularly since Vatican II, in 'the universal call to holiness'. The how of this call in relation to the tower metaphor is explained more fully by Keating.

'All Possession' of the 'False Self' has to be Surrendered Completely

The transforming challenge as presented by Keating is to negate the 'false self'. Cassian teaches abandonment of all 'self-possession' in absolute trust and dependence on God 'in purity of heart' as the foundation of the spiritual journey. Keating gives the meaning of self here as *sarx*, a Greek word meaning the 'false self' which is of our own creating, as opposed to *soma* the Greek word which means one's 'true self' open to growth and transformation 'in Christ'.[28] This meaning has been lost to many modern readers due to the limitations in translation.

With regard to the meaning of words it is interesting to note that words used by Cassian like 'faults' and 'vices' have almost, if not completely disappeared off our behaviour radar screen but 'addictions' and 'compulsions' are *in* big time. It is the possession of the 'false self' that has to be completely surrendered, 'given up' or 'cut off'[29] in order to enable our 'true self' to emerge,[30] rise up and follow Christ into a 'new dimension of being',[31] Because it is 'the 'false self' that is the cause of our spiritual retardation.[32] Keating states that the 'false self' is:

> Developed in our own likeness rather than in the likeness of God, and thus the distortion of the image of God in which we are created. The *false-self* seeks happiness in the 'emotional programmes' of gratifying the instinctual needs of *survival/security*, *affection/esteem*, and *power/control*, and bases its self-worth and identity on *cultural* and *group identification*.[33] [Emphasis added]

Keating also gives us helpful insights from modern psychology of how the 'false self' is brought about in developing these 'emotional programmes' for happiness from early childhood in order to cope with trauma or frustration. Where these programmes are pursued into adulthood, they can never satisfy the human heart, and when frustrated set off afflictive emotions. These he names as 'greed, lust, anger, envy, grief, fear, pride, and apathy', a list almost identical with Cassian's list of 'universal faults'.[34]

There is a clear parallel with Cassian's paired faults, of gluttony and fornication, avarice and anger, vainglory and pride, and Keating's 'emotional programmes' of survival/security, affection/esteem and power/control, respectively. These have to be given up, 'eradicated', or as Jesus says 'cut off',[35] for the building up of the 'tower walls of virtue' of the 'true-self' for entry, into the joy and rest of God.

For establishing a life of virtue, Keating summarises Cassian's 'remedies' with his clarion *remedy* call from the Scriptures *Repent*[36] explained by Keating to mean 'Change the direction in which you are looking for Happiness'.[37] It is the first word spoken by Jesus in Mark's Gospel. Jesus emerges from the desert, 'led by the Spirit' with the Scriptures as his breastplate, having overcome the universal temptations of all humankind to the self-indulgence of instinctual needs on which one cannot live alone in the first; resisting the temptation to possessive greed and avarice in the second; and finally to the temptation in a hero display of self-glorification of vanity and pride in the third.[38] Jesus, the 'Divine Therapist'[39] demonstrates to all who would wish to follow Him that only when these 'emotional temptations' of the 'false self' are recognised and eradicated, is one free to develop a deep relationship with God, and with all others within this relationship, which is the sole purpose of His mission.[40]

Lectio divina: Awaking to a New Dimension of Life

What Keating has to say about *lectio divina* and indeed the whole spiritual journey offers new insights to our reflection on this matter of growth and transformation in relation to the tower teaching. He highlights the relationship aspect of this prayer by comparing and paralleling the four main levels of growth in relationship with a friend, with the four levels or stages of growth in one's relationship with God through *lectio divina,* echoing Cassian's 'little by little' growth into intimacy with God.[41]

He demonstrates the growth process from first acquaintance in reading, to developing friendship through reflection, and from deepening one's bond in prayer, and finally to the intimacy of rest in God's presence and love. This 'rest in God', experienced by the humble of heart is not, as Keating explains, a week or month under a heavenly palm tree. It is to experience the peace and reign of God in one's heart, in a 'new dimension of life',[42] achieved by Christ on the Cross for all humankind and gifted to all who 'follow Him' by participating in His life of self-emptying Love.

Keating, building on all the previous developments of this form of prayer, takes it a stage further which has special significance for our time, in relation to our tower metaphor. He compares the model of the Christian Spiritual Journey through *lectio divina* with the evolutionary model in new higher levels of human consciousness.[43] He demonstrates how this spiritual journey facilitates the evolvement out of egotistic centred love in enslavement to the 'false self' and its emotional programmes for happiness, to the 'true self' which 'opens the door to higher states of consciousness namely "Christ Consciousness",[44] a new dimension of life which Jesus has realised for us through his Resurrection'.[45] Keating states that our human potentialities are only fully realised in this transforming union, through prayer in the 'innermost being of the heart',[46] which as Cassian explains is God's Gift to all persevere to the 'uppermost cone of the tower', in the innermost abode of one's heart (Mt 6:6).[47]

Contemplative Living: The Unfolding of Christ's Resurrection in all Humankind

The challenge of Christian discipleship experienced, through the process of *lectio divina*, culminates in the experience of contemplative prayer and living, and is equivalent to Eucharistic Living at its deepest meaning. Keating urges one, in the words of St Augustine, 'To receive the Eucharist in order to become the Eucharist.' This awakening to the presence and action of the spirit is the unfolding of Christ's Resurrection in us, and the peak of mysticism.[48] Pope Benedict XVI has awakened the Church today to this, as the real challenge of the Eucharist.[49] And he states, this new dimension of being which Jesus realised for humankind through his Cross and Resurrection, and celebrated at every Eucharist:

> Is not just some miracle from the past, the occurrence of which could be ultimately a matter of indifference to [humankind]: It is a qualitative leap in the history of

> 'evolution' and of life in general towards a new future life, towards a new world which, starting from Christ, already continuously permeates this world of ours, transforms it and draws it to itself.[50]

Only by 'becoming what we receive' by renouncing possession of the 'false self' in a spirit of complete detachment, can one realise one's true self-identity in Christ as the Beloved of God and through Christ our unity and communion with all other human beings.

This challenge of personal evolutionary growth and transformation is what the sublime tower icon offers not only to the monks and Christians of our day, but to all humankind. It is the way upward in Christ towards the 'New Heavens and New Earth'. As the Scriptures proclaim: 'What we are waiting for is what God has promised: the new heavens and new earth, the place where righteousness will be at home.'[51] This righteousness means right relationship in a 'New Springtime in the Church' predicted by Pope John Paul II, hastening the fulfilment of it with one's God, self, neighbour, environment, and cosmos.[52] Keating claims that 'one of the things that prayer, as it deepens will affect, is our intuition, with regard to the oneness of the human race, and, indeed, the oneness of all creation'.[53] This would certainly help hasten the fulfilment of Christ's last prayer, 'May they all be One, Father … as You are in Me and I am in You' (Jn 17:21).

Bringing together now these considerations, I conclude by proposing that there is a strong case to assert that as well as functioning as an 'anchorite tower',[54] 'a bell-tower for the call to prayer'[55] and possibly many other of the proposed uses.[56] The original purpose in building 'the sublime round tower' in its unique architectural design was to serve as a three-dimensional iconic call to contemplative prayer through lived discipleship according to Cassian's teaching on (Lk 14:33).[57]

In the present time of confusion, search and evolving consciousness,[58] 'the appointed time' is now to reclaim this 'Spiritual Heritage' in renewed attention to this iconic call. It could with more urgency than ever, awaken or reawaken the human heart, to a radical response of discipleship in lived Eucharistic self-emptying love (Ph 2:3–5). Taken seriously, Pope Benedict XVI argues, this can change the world – indeed, it's the only thing that can,[59] and exemplified by Pope Francis, leading all to live 'continuously in the divine Presence',[60] and, coming to know 'the love of Christ, which is beyond knowledge and to be filled with the utter fullness of God' (Ep 3:19). 'May God who has begun this work … bring it to completion' (Ph 1:6), as we reclaim with renewed earnestness the path of those who have blazed the trail before us, and expressed in such earnest prayer embedded in the ancient Irish prayer, years before it was composed as a hymn:

Be Thou my Vision, O Lord of my Heart

Be Thou my breastplate, my sword for the fight;
Be Thou my whole armour, be Thou my true might;
Be Thou my soul's shelter, be Thou my *high tower*:
Raise Thou me heavenward, great Power of my power.[61]
[Emphasis added]

Notes

Introduction

1. D.L. Walker, trans., *John Cassian* (unpublished copyright work, Educational Centre for Christian Spirituality, Randwick, Australia), *c.*1986. David is now Bishop of Broken Bay, NSW Australia. For his full biography see, www.dbb.org.au/ourdiocese (2012).
2. See S. Schneiders, 'Spirituality in the Academy', *Theological Studies*, 50 (1989), 676–97 at 687.
3. See B. Lalor, *The Irish Round Tower Origins and Architecture Explored* (Cork: The Collins Press, 1999), 13.
4. Pope Benedict XVI, *The Lenten Journey: Words for Lent and Easter* (London: CTS, 2007), 28. See also *Easter Vigil Homily of his Holiness Benedict XVI*, 2006, http://www.vatican.va/holy_father/benedict_xvi/homilies/2006/documents/hf_ben-xvi (2011).
5. Pope Benedict XVI, *The Lenten Journey: Words for Lent and Easter*, (London: CTS, 2007), op. cit., 29.
6. A. Flannery, ed., Vatican Council II, *The Conciliar and Post Conciliar Documents* (New York: Costello Pub. Co., 1977), 396.
7. T. Keating, *Manifesting God* (New York: Lantern books, 2005), 113. A complete list of Thomas Keating's work can be accessed on website, http://www.goodreads.com/author/list/30607.Thomas_Keating.
8. F. Chiovaro, 'Cassian, John (Johannes Cassianus)', *New Catholic Encyclopedia* (NCE), 3 (Washington: Catholic University of America, Thomson-Gale, 2003), 205–7 at 205.
9. F. Bordonali, 'Cassian, John, in A. Di Berardino, ed., *Encyclopaedia of the Early Church*, vol. I (Cambridge: James Clark & Co., Ltd, 1992), 149.
10. F. Chiovaro, op. cit., NCE 3, 207.
11. O. Chadwick, *John Cassian* (Cambridge: University Press, 1950), 7.
12. O. Chadwick, *John Cassian* (Cambridge: University Press, 1968), 92.

13 Ibid., 154.

14 J. Cassian, *Conf.* 1.1 in the edition by H. Wace and P. Schaff, *A Select Library of Nicene and Post-Nicene Fathers,* vol. XI (NPNF) (Oxford: James Parker and Company, New York: The Christian Literature Company, 1894), 295.

15 See *Conf.* 1.5 (NPNF, 296).

16 J.J. Levko, *Cassian's Prayer for the 21st Century* (Scranton: The University of Scranton Press, 2000), 74.

17 *Conf.* 1.4 (NPNF, 296).

18 Ibid.

19 C. Stewart, *Cassian the Monk* (Oxford University Press, 1998), 86.

20 Ibid., 96.

21 *Conf.* 1.13 (NPNF, 300).

22 C. Stewart, op. cit., 96.

23 See *Conf.* 10.6 (NPNF, 403).

24 J. Cassian, op. cit., *Institutes of John Cassian,* 12.33 (NPNF, 290).

25 O. Chadwick, op. cit. (1968 edition), 151.

26 *Inst.* 4.43 (NPNF, 233).

27 *Conf.* 9.2 (NPNF, 387).

28 Ibid.

29 *Conf.* 1.6 (NPNF, 297).

30 *Conf.* 9.2 (NPNF, 387).

Chapter One

1 *Inst.* 12.3 (NPNF, 290).

2 C. Stewart, op. cit., 205.

3 *Conf.* 19.2 (NPNF, 387).

4 Ibid.

5 *Conf.* 19.2 (NPNF, 490).

6 *Conf.* 15.7 (NPNF, 448).

7 M. Casey, *Apatheia*, in M. Downey, ed., *The New Dictionary of Catholic Spirituality* (NDCS) (Collegeville/Minnesota: The Liturgical Press, A Michael Glazier Book, 1993), 50.

8 See C. Stewart, op. cit., 46.

9 *Conf.* 1.6 (NPNF, 297).

10 *Inst.* 4.32 (NPNF, 230).

11 *Inst.* 4.33 (NPNF, 230).
12 *Inst.* 4.43 (NPNF, 233).
13 T. Keating, *Intimacy with God* (New York: Crossroad Publishing Company, 2005), 30.
14 *Conf.* 9.2 (NPNF, 387).
15 *Conf.* 9.3 (NPNF, 388).
16 See *Inst.* 4.43 (NPNF, 233).
17 C. Stewart, op. cit., 123.
18 *Inst.* 4.3 (NPNF, 230).
19 T. Keating, *Manifesting God,* op. cit., 1.
20 *Conf.* 3.6 (NPNF, 321).
21 C. Luibheid, trans., *John Cassian Conferences*, Classics of Western Spirituality (New York/Mahwah: Paulist Press, 1985), 85.
22 Ibid.
23 *Inst.* 4.35 (NPNF, 231).
24 *Conf.* 3.7 (NPNF, 323).
25 The Scripture quotation here is from the Cassian's text (NPNF, 325).
26 *Conf.* 15.7 (NPNF, 448).

Chapter Two

1 *Inst.* 4.43 (NPNF, 233).
2 *Conf.* 9.2 (NPNF, 387).
3 See *Conf.* 9.4 (NPNF, 388).
4 *Inst.* 4.43 (NPNF, 233).
5 See *Conf.* 9.2 (NPNF, 387).
6 *Conf.* 1.5 (NPNF, 297).
7 C. Stewart, op. cit., 107.
8 See *Conf.* 5.2 (NPNF, 339); *Inst.* 5.1 (NPNF, 233).
9 G. Evans, *Deadly Sins*, in M. Downey, ed., NDCS, 248.
10 *Inst.* 5.5 (NPNF, 235); *Conf.* 9.5 (NPNF, 389).
11 *Conf.* 5.10 (NPNF, 343).
12 *Conf.* 5.10 (NPNF, 343).
13 *Inst.* 5.13 (NPNF, 238).
14 *Inst.* 7.2 (NPNF, 249).
15 *Inst.* 7.21 (NPNF, 255).
16 *Conf.* 5.11 (NPNF, 344).

[17] *Inst.* 8.22 (NPNF, 263).
[18] *Conf.* 18.13 (NPNF, 484).
[19] *Inst.* 7.2 (NPNF, 250).
[20] *Conf.* 5.4 (NPNF, 340).
[21] *Conf.* 19.2 (NPNF, 490).
[22] *Inst.* 8.17 (NPNF, 262).
[23] C. Stewart, op. cit., 66.
[24] *Inst.* 9.1 (NPNF, 264).
[25] M. Casey, *Acedia,* in M. Downey, ed., NDCS, 4.
[26] *Inst.* 10.3 (NPNF, 267).
[27] *Conf.* 1.4 (NPNF, 296).
[28] *Conf.* 9.2 (NPNF, 387).
[29] *Inst.* 10.1 (NPNF, 266).
[30] *Inst.* 10.2 (NPNF, 267).
[31] *Inst.* 10.6 (NPNF, 268).
[32] *Inst.* 10.3 (NPNF, 267).
[33] *Inst.*, ibid.
[34] *Conf.* 9.2 (NPNF, 387).
[35] *Conf.* 5.10 (NPNF, 343).
[36] The Scripture quotations here are from Cassian's text (NPNF, 268 and 269 respectively).
[37] *Inst.* 10.7 (NPNF, 268).
[38] *Inst.* 10.7 (NPNF, 269).
[39] *Inst.* 10.3 (NPNF, 267).
[40] *Inst.* 10.7 (NPNF, 269).
[41] *Inst.* 10.14 (NPNF, 271).
[42] *Conf.* 2.4 (NPNF, 310).
[43] *Inst.* 12.31 (NPNF, 290).
[44] *Conf.* 5.10 (NPNF, 343).
[45] Ibid.
[46] *Conf.* 5.7 (NPNF, 342).
[47] *Inst.* 12.3 (NPNF, 280).
[48] *Inst.* 12.4 (NPNF, 281).
[49] C. Stewart, op. cit., 66. See *Inst.* 12.9 (NPNF, 282).
[50] *Inst.* 11.8 (NPNF, 277).
[51] *Conf.* 2.4 (NPNF, 310).
[52] *Conf.* 2.2 (NPNF, 309).

53 *Inst.* 11.19 (NPNF, 279).
54 *Inst.* 12.32 (NPNF, 290).
55 *Inst.* 12.31 (NPNF, 290).
56 C. Stewart, op. cit., 83. See *Conf.* 9.3 (NPNF, 388).

Chapter Three

1 H.D. Egan, *An Anthology of Christian Mysticism* (A Pueblo Book, Minnesota: The Liturgical Press, 1996), 14.
2 D.L. Walker, trans., *John Cassian*, op. cit., *Conf.* 9.2.
3 C. Stewart, op. cit., 43.
4 *Conf.* 9.2 (NPNF, 388).
5 *Conf.* 9.2 (NPNF, 387).
6 H.D. Egan, op. cit., 72.
7 *Conf.* 9.3 (NPNF, 388).
8 Ibid.
9 *Conf.* 9.8 (NPNF, 390).
10 *Conf.* 9.15 (NPNF, 392).
11 *Conf.* 9.17 (NPNF, 393).
12 C. Stewart, op. cit., 108.
13 *Conf.* 9.16 (NPNF, 392).
14 *Conf.* 9.3 (NPNF, 388).
15 *Conf.* 2.4 (NPNF, 310).
16 *Conf.* 9.2 (NPNF, 387).
17 C. Stewart, op. cit., 35.
18 K.W. Irwin, *Lectio Divina*, in M. Downey, ed. (NDCS, 596.).
19 C. Stewart, op. cit., 113.
20 *Conf.* 5.4 (NPNF, 340), *Conf.* 5.15 (NPNF, 346), *Conf.* 10.10 (NPNF, 205–7), *Conf.* 14.10 (NPNF, 439–440).
21 C. Stewart, op. cit., 73.
22 Ibid., 101.
23 K.W. Irwin, op. cit., 596.
24 *Conf.* 9.3 (NPNF, 388), *Conf.* 9.16 (NPNF, 392).
25 *Conf.* 9.2 (NPNF, 387).
26 *Conf.* 9.18 (NPNF, 393).
27 Ibid.
28 C. Stewart, op. cit., 109.

[29] *Conf.* 9.24 (NPNF, 296).
[30] *Conf.* 9.19 (NPNF, 394).
[31] *Conf.* 10.7 (NPNF, 404).
[32] *Conf.* 19.2 (NPNF, 400).
[33] D.L. Walker, trans., *Conf.* 9.25.
[34] Ibid.
[35] *Conf.* 9.27 (NPNF, 396).
[36] *Conf.* 9.32 (NPNF, 398).
[37] R.E. Brown, J.A. Fitzmyer, R.E. Murphy, eds. *The Jerome Biblical Commentary* (JBC) (London: Geoffrey Chapman, 1990), NT 41:6. See J. Main, *Community of Love* (London: DLT 1990), 108, and H.U. von Balthasar, *Prayer*, A.V. Littledale, trans. (London: SPCK 1973), 29, 31.
[38] A. Jones, ed. (NJB, Mt 8:10, footnote b).
[39] Ibid.
[40] *Conf.* 9.34 (NPNF, 399).
[41] *Conf.* 9.25 (NPNF, 396).
[42] D.L. Walker, trans., op. cit., *Conf.* 9.35.
[43] C. Stewart, op. cit., 108.
[44] *Conf.* 1.22 (NPNF, 306).
[45] *Conf.* 10.7 (NPNF, 404).
[46] C. Stewart, op. cit., 109.
[47] Ibid., 113.
[48] C. Stewart, op. cit., 130.
[49] *Conf.* 10.6 (NPNF, 403).
[50] *Conf.* 10.7 (NPNF, 404).
[51] Ibid.
[52] *Conf.* 10.8 (NPNF, 404).
[53] Ibid.
[54] *Conf.* 9.36 (NPNF, 400).
[55] *Conf.* 10.9 (NPNF, 405).
[56] Ibid.
[57] Ibid.
[58] The Scripture translation here is taken from H.D. Egan, op. cit., 72.
[59] D.L. Walker, trans., *Conf.* 10.10, op. cit.
[60] C. Luibheid, trans., *John Cassian Conferences*, in the *Introduction* by O. Chadwick, Classics of Western Spirituality, op. cit., 13.

61 I. Zaleski, Living the Jesus Prayer (Canada: Novalis & Gracewing, 1997), 1–3.

62 H.D. Egan, op. cit., 72.

63 D.L. Walker, *A commentary on the Tenth Conference on Prayer* (unpublished lecture copyright), op. cit. The formula is still recited in Latin in many monasteries as follows: *Deus, in adjutorium meum intende, Domine, ad adiuvandum me festina.* See an Irish hymn adaptation of this beautiful prayer at the end of this chapter.

64 *Conf.* 10.10 (NPNF, 406).

65 K. Hughes, *The Church in Early Irish Society*, St Patrick's Breastplate (London: Methuen & Co. Ltd, 1966), 164.

66 *Conf.* 10.10 (NPNF, 406).

67 *Conf.* 10.10 (NPNF, 407).

68 *Conf.* 10.14, trans., D.L. Walker.

69 *Conf.* 1.18 (NPNF, 303).

70 *Conf.* 10.11 (NPNF, 407).

71 *Conf.* 10.10 (NPNF, 406).

72 *Conf.* 10.11 (NPNF, 407).

73 *Conf.* 10.11 (NPNF, 408).

74 *Conf.* 10.10 (NPNF, 407).

75 *Conf.* 10.7 (NPNF, 404). See also H.U. von Balthasar, op. cit., 149.

76 Ibid.

77 *Conf.* 10.8 (NPNF, 404).

78 Ibid.

79 *Conf.* 10.14 (NPNF, 409).

80 *Conf.* 10.11 (NPNF, 407).

81 I. Zaleski, Living the Jesus Prayer (Canada: Novalis & Gracewing, 1997), 1; also, *The Cloud of Unknowing*, ch. 7.

82 G. Murphy, *Early Irish Lyrics: Eighth to Twelfth Centuries* (Dublin 1998), 52–9, www.irishlyrics.ie (Feb. 2012). Note, this hymn is in Latin and Irish, indicating the understanding and frequency of the use of the initial prayer formula.

Chapter Four

1 D.L. Walker, trans., op. cit.

2 O. Chadwick, op. cit., 36.

3 C. Stewart, op. cit., 18.

4 H. G. J. Beck, '*Honoratus of Arles, St*,' NCE7 (Washington: Catholic University of America, Thomson-Gale, 2003) 79.

5 O. Chadwick, op. cit., 148.

6 J. Ryan, *Irish Monasticism, Origins and Early Developments* (Shannon Ireland: Irish University Press, 1972), 407.

7 Translation by L. de Paor, *St Patrick's World, The Christian Culture of Ireland's Apostolic Age* (Dublin: Four Courts Press, 1993), 40.

8 Ibid., 79.

9 L. de Paor, op. cit., 202.

10 J. Ryan, *Irish Monasticism, Origins and Early Developments*, op. cit., 64–7.

11 Ibid., 407.

12 Ibid., 64.

13 Ibid., 67.

14 Ibid., 64.

15 Ibid., 102.

16 Ibid., 328.

17 O. Davies, ed., with T. O' Loughlin's collaboration, *Celtic Spirituality*, Classic of Western Spirituality (New York Mahweh: Paulist Press, 1999), 37–40.

18 N. Chadwick, 'The Early Church in the British Isles, and the Continental and Eastern Background (Fifth Century)' in *The Age of the Saints in the Early Celtic Church*, Felinfach: Llanerch Publishers [1960] (Facsimile Reprint), 1–60 at 50.

19 C. Luibheid, trans., *John Cassian Conferences*, in the *Introduction* by O. Chadwick, Classics of Western Spirituality, op. cit., 32 ff.

20 J. Ryan, op. cit., 328.

21 Ibid., 331–2.

22 Ibid., 408.

23 Ibid., 260.

24 Ibid., 219–20.

25 Ibid., 332.

26 Ibid., 260.

27 W. Horn, J. W. Marshall, G. D. Rourke, *The Forgotten Hermitage of Skellig Michael* (Berkley: University of California Press, *c.*1990) 76 http://www.ark.cdlib.org/ark:13030/ft1d5n0gb.

28 K. Hughes, *The Church in Early Irish Society*, op. cit., 173–6.

29 W. Horn, J.W. Marshall, G.D. Rourke, *The Forgotten Hermitage of Skellig Michael,* op. cit., 77.

30 O. Davis, op. cit., 60.

31 B. Lalor, *The Irish Round Tower Origins and Architecture Explored*, op. cit., 90.

32 G.L. Barrow, op. cit., 176.

33 Ibid.

34 G.L. Barrow, *Irish Round Towers*, Irish Heritage Series 8 (Dublin: Eason and Son Ltd, 1976), 2.

35 G.P. Petrie, *The Ecclesiastical Architecture of Ireland, anterior to the Anglo-Norman invasion; comprising an essay on the origin and uses of the round towers of Ireland, which obtained the gold medal prize of the Royal Irish Academy* (Dublin: Hodges and Smith, 1845), 2.

36 Ibid.

37 G.L. Barrow, *The Round Towers of Ireland: A Study and Gazetteer* (Dublin: The Academy Press, 1979), 35.

38 K. Hughes, *The Church in Early Irish Society*, op. cit., 236.

39 B. Lalor, op. cit., 15.

40 J. Ryan, op. cit., 413.

41 K. Hughes, *The Church in Early Irish Society*, op. cit., 236.

42 B. Lalor, *The Irish Round Tower Origins and Architecture Explored*, op. cit., 15.

43 R. Stalley, *Irish Round Towers*, The Irish Treasures Series (Dublin: County House, 2000), 14–16.

44 T. O'Loughlin, *Celtic Theology: Humanity, World and God in early Irish Writings* (London and New York, 2000), 167.

45 R. Hitchcock, *Notes on the Round Towers, and some other antiquities of the county of Kerry, from the Transactions of the Kilkenny Archaeological Society, for the year 1853* (Dublin: Printed by John O'Daly, 9, Anglesea-street, 1854), 7 with footnote 2. See also http://www.sacred-texts.com/pag/idr/31.htm, 270.

46 D. O' Byrne, *The History of the round towers of Ireland* (Kilkenny: Printed at the Journal Office, Parade, 1877), 5.

47 G.P. Petrie, *The Ecclesiastical Architecture of Ireland*, op. cit., 2.

48 B. Lalor, *The Irish Round Tower Origins and Architecture Explored*, op. cit., 16–17.

49 Ibid., 17.

50 R. Stalley, *Irish Round Towers*, The Irish Treasures Series, op. cit., 7.

[51] Ibid., 33–5.
[52] NJB, op. cit., 2P 3:13, see also Is 65:17, Rv 21:1.
[53] M. Ryan, series editor of *The Irish Treasures Series*, R. Stalley, op. cit., on the cover review of this work.

Chapter Five

[1] H.D. Egan, op. cit., 6. Also H.U. von Balthasar, op. cit., 149, and Abhisiktánanda, *Prayer* (New Delhi: ISPCK 1993), 117–19.
[2] 50th International Eucharistic Congress, 2012 *The Eucharist: Communion With Christ and With One Another* (Dublin: Veritas Publications 2011), 54–8, www.iec2012.ie.
[3] Pope John Paul II, *Novo Millennio Ineunte, At the Beginning of the New Millennium*, Apostolic Letter (London: CTS, 2001), 28, No. 30.
[4] John Paul II, *L'Osservatore Romano*, Rome, 2 Feb. 1988. I am indebted to Fr Pat Murray SCA for this reference.
[5] O. Chadwick, op. cit., 161.
[6] See D.H. Egan, op. cit., *passim*.
[7] See www.newmonasticismireland.org (2012) and associated websites.
[8] D.H. Egan, op. cit., 2, 77.
[9] Mt 10:37–9; Mk 8:34–5; Lk 9:23–5; Jn 12:25.
[10] Mt 3:2, footnote b. NJB.
[11] A. Flannery, ed., Vatican Council II, *The Conciliar and Post Conciliar Documents*, op. cit., G. S., no. 4.
[12] Pope John Paul II, *Novo Millennio Ineunte, At the Beginning of the New Millennium*, op. cit., 31.
[13] B. Griffiths, *The New Creation in Christ*, Christian Meditation and Community (London: DLT. 1992), 1–12.
[14] B. Griffiths, A New Vision of Reality (London: Fount 1989), chaps 2 and 13. Also D. Ó Murchú, *Prophetic Horizons of Religious Life* (London: Escalibur Press, 1989), 56.
[15] T. Keating, *Better Part,* in foreward by L. Freeman OSB (New York London: The Continuum International Publishing Group Inc., 2009), 14.
[16] B. Griffiths, *The New Creation in Christ*, op. cit., 77.
[17] A. Flannery, ed., Vatican Council II, *The Conciliar and Post Conciliar Documents*, op. cit., L.G., no. 40, 396. See also John Paul II, *Novo*

Millennio Ineunte, At the Beginning of the New Millennium, op. cit., 28, no. 29.

[18] J. Main, *The Inner Christ* (London: DLT, 1987), 39, 40.

[19] Pope John Paul II, *Novo Millennio Ineunte, At the Beginning of the New Millennium,* op. cit., 31, no. 33.

[20] Pope John Paul II, *Tertio Millennio Adveniente, As the Third Millennium Draws Near* (London: CTS, 1994), 53, no. 40.

[21] A good resource for contemplative living: www.contemplativeoutreach.org (Aug. 2012).

[22] A good resource for Christian Meditation: www.chrstianmeditation.org.uk (Aug. 2012).

[23] R. Rohr, see www.cacradicalgrace.org (May 2012).

[24] R. Rohr, *The Naked Now* (New York: The Crossroad Publishing Company, 2009), 114, footnote 50.

[25] A complete list of Thomas Keating's work can be accessed on website, http://www.goodreads.com/author/list/30607.Thomas_Keating.

[26] T. Keating, *Manifesting God*, op. cit., 129.

[27] T. Keating, *Open Mind, Open Heart* (New York, London: The Continuum International Publishing Group Inc., 2009). For the method of centring prayer, 175–81.

[28] T. Keating, *The Mystery of Christ, The Liturgy as Spiritual Experience* (New York, London: The Continuum International Publishing Group Inc., 2005), 26.

[29] T. Keating, *Invitation to Love. The way of Christian Contemplation* (New York, London: The Continuum International Publishing Group Inc., 2007), 11, 47.

[30] Ibid., 48.

[31] Pope Benedict XVI, *The Lenten Journey: Words for Lent and Easter* (London: CTS, 2007), 28. See also *Easter Vigil Homily of his Holiness Benedict XVI*, 2006, op. cit., http://www.vatican.va/holy_father/benedict_xvi/homilies/2006/documents/hf_ben xvi (2011).

[32] T. Keating, *Manifesting God,* op. cit., 38.

[33] T. Keating, *Open Mind, Open Heart*, op. cit., 187 and 2.

[34] T. Keating. *Invitation to Love: The way of Christian Contemplation*, op. cit., 20.

[35] Ibid., 11.

[36] NJB, op. cit., Mt 3:2 footnote c.

[37] T. Keating, *Manifesting God*, op. cit., 1: *The Mystery of Christ, The Liturgy as Spiritual Experience*, op. cit., 37.

[38] NJB, op. cit., Mk 1:12–13, Lk 4:1–13, Mt 4:1–13, see also footnote a.

[39] T. Keating, *Manifesting God*, op. cit., 93.

[40] Ibid., ix.

[41] T. Keating, *Intimacy with God*, op. cit., 33.

[42] Pope Benedict XVI, *The Lenten Journey: Words for Lent and Easter*, op. cit., 28.

[43] T. Keating, This comparison is addressed comprehensively in *Invitation to Love. The way of Christian Contemplation*, op. cit., *passim*, but a good summary can be accessed on www.thomaskeating/levels of consciousness/definitions.

[44] T. Keating, *The Mystery of Christ: The Liturgy as Spiritual Experience*, op. cit., 27 and 97–9.

[45] Pope Benedict XVI, *The Lenten Journey: Words for Lent and Easter*, op. cit., 30.

[46] T. Keating, *Heart of the World* (New York: Crossroad Publishing Company, 2008), 77.

[47] See Cassian, on *The Prayer of complete Silence,* chapter 3.

[48] T. Keating, *Manifesting God*, op. cit., 34–5.

[49] J.L. Allen, Jr, *10 Things Pope Benedict Wants You to Know*, CTS (2007), 18–19.

[50] Pope Benedict XVI, *The Lenten Journey: Words for Lent and Easter*, op. cit., 28.

[51] Jerusalem Bible, op. cit., 2P 3:13, see also Is 65:17, Rv 21:1.

[52] I am indebted for this insight, to Ruth Patterson from the Anglican Communion at a Charismatic Convention (Athlone, 2006).

[53] T. Keating, *Heart of the World*, op. cit., 77.

[54] G.P. Petrie, *The Ecclesiastical Architecture of Ireland, anterior to the Anglo-Norman invasion; comprising an essay on the origin and uses of the round towers of Ireland, which obtained the gold medal prize of the Royal Irish Academy*, op. cit., 2.

[55] T. O'Loughlin, *Celtic Theology: Humanity, World and God in early Irish Writings*, op. cit., 167.

[56] B. Lalor, op. cit., 67–71.

[57] This insight was endorsed by Brian Lalor, author of *The Irish Round Tower, Origins and Architecture Explored*, 31 March 2004, op. cit.

[58] T. Keating, *The Mystery of Christ: The Liturgy as Spiritual Experience*, op. cit., 27.

[59] J.L. Allen, Jr, *10 Things Pope Benedict Wants You to Know*, op. cit., 19.

[60] T. Keating, *Manifesting God*, op. cit., 70–80 at 80.

[61] From the original Irish *Bí Thusa' mo Shúile,* trans. by M.E. Byrne 1905, versified by E.H. Hull, 1912. 'The text had been a part of Irish Monastic tradition for centuries before its setting to the tune, therefore, before it became an actual hymn.' See: http://en.wikipedia.org/wiki/Be_Thou_My_Vision.

Bibliography

PRIMARY SOURCES

Keating, T., *Manifesting God* (New York: Lantern books, 2005).

Liubheid, C., trans., *John Cassian Conferences*, The Classics of Western Spirituality (New York/Mahweh: Paulist Press, 1985).

Ryan, J., *Irish Monasticism, Origins and Early Development* (Shannon, Ireland: Irish University Press, 1972).

Wace, H., and Schaff, P., trans., *The Works of John Cassian,* in: *A Select Library of Nicene and Post-Nicene Fathers* (NPNF), vol. XI (Oxford: James Parker and Company, New York: The Christian Literature Company, 1894).

Walker, D. L., trans., *John Cassian* (unpublished work: copyright), Christian Spirituality Educational Centre, Randwick, Australia, *c.*1986. David is now Bishop of Broken Bay, NSW Australia, for his full biography see, www.dbb.org.au/ourdiocese (2011).

SECONDARY SOURCES

Abhishiktánanda, *Prayer* (New Delhi: ISPCK, 1993).

Allen, Jr, J. L. *10 Things Pope Benedict Wants You to Know* (London: CTS, 2007).

Balthasar, H. U. von, *Prayer*, trans. A. V. Littledale (London: SPCK 1973).

Barrow, G. L., *The Round Towers of Ireland* (Dublin: The Academy Press, 1979).

Barrow, G. L., *Irish Round Towers*, The Irish Heritage Series 8 (Dublin: Eason and Son Ltd, 1976).

Benedict XVI, Pope; *The Lenten Journey: Words for Lent and Easter* London: CTS, 2007. See *Easter Vigil Homily of his Holiness Benedict XVI*, 2006, http://www.vatican.va/holy_father/benedict_xvi/homilies/2006/documents/hf_ben-xvi.

Chadwick, O., *John Cassian* (Cambridge: University Press, 1950 and 1968).

Davis, O., in collaboration with T. O'Loughlin eds, *Celtic Spirituality* (New York/Mahweh: Paulist Press, 1999).

de Paor, L., trans., *St Patrick's World, The Christian Culture of Ireland's Apostolic Age* (Dublin: Four Courts Press, 1993).

Egan, H.D., *An Anthology of Christian Mysticism*, Pueblo Books (Collegeville, Minnesota: The Liturgical Press, 1996).

A. Flannery, ed., Vatican Council II, *The Conciliar and Post Conciliar Documents* (New York: Costello Pub. Co., 1977).

Griffiths, B., *New Vision of Reality* (London: Fount, 1989).

Griffiths, B., *The New Creation in Christ*, Meditation and Community (London: DLT, 1992).

Horn, W., Marshall, J.W., Rourke, G.D., *The Forgotten Hermitage of Skellig Michael* (Berkley: University of California Press, 1990).

International Eucharistic Congress 50th, 2012 *The Eucharist: Communion: with Christ and with One Another* (Dublin: Veritas Publications, 2011), www.iec2012.ie.

John Paul II, Pope, *Tertio Millennio Adveniente, As the Third Millennium Draws Near, Apostolic Letter* (London: CTS, 1994).

John Paul II, Pope, *Novo Millennio Ineunte, At the Beginning of the New Millennium, Apostolic Letter* (London: CTS, 2001).

Keating, T., *Manifesting God* (New York: Lantern books, 2005).

Keating, T., *Intimacy with God* (New York: Crossroad Publishing Company, 2005).

Keating, T., *The Mystery of Christ, The Liturgy as Spiritual Experience* (New York, London: The Continuum International Publishing Group Inc., 2005).

Keating, T., *Invitation to Love: The Way of Christian Contemplation* (New York, London: The Continuum International Publishing Group Inc., 2007).

Keating, T., *Open Mind, Open Heart* (New York: London: The Continuum International Publishing Group Inc., 2009).

Keating, T., *Heart of the World* (New York: Crossroad Publishing Company, 2008).

Keating, T., *Open Mind, Open Heart* (New York, London: The Continuum International Publishing Group Inc., 2009).

Keating, T., *Better Part* (New York, London: The Continuum International Publishing Group Inc., 2009).

A complete list of Thomas Keating's work; see http://www.goodreads.com/author/list/30607.Thomas_Keating.

Lalor, B., *The Irish Round Tower, Origins and Architecture Explored* (Dublin: The Colins Press, 1999).

Levko, J.J., *Cassian's Prayer for the 21st Century* (Scranton: The University of Seranton Press, 2000).

Main, J., *Word into Silence* (London: DLT, 1985).

Main, J., *Community of Love* (London: DLT, 1990).

Main, J., *The Inner Christ* (London: DLT, 1987).

O'Murchú, D., *Prophetic Horizons of Religious Life* (London: Excalibur Press, 1989).

Rohr, R., *The Naked Now* (New York: Crossroad Publishing Company, 2009).

Stalley, R., *Irish Round Towers,* The Irish Treasures Series (Dublin: County House, 2000).

Stewart, C., *Cassian the Monk* (Oxford: University Press, 1998).

Zaleski, I., *Living the Jesus Prayer* (Canada: Novalis and Gracewing, 1997).

ARTICLES

Bordonali, F., 'Cassian John': in A. Di Berardino, ed., *Encyclopedia of the Early Church*, vol. I (Cambridge: James Clark and Co. Ltd, 1992), 149.

Casey, M., 'Acedia', in M. Downey, ed., *The New Dictionary of Catholic Spirituality*, NDCS (Collegeville, Minnesota: The Liturgical Press, 1993), 4.

Casey, M., 'Apatheia', in M. Downey, ed., NDCS, 50.

Chadwick, N., 'The Early Church in the British Isles, and the Continental and Eastern Background' (Fifth Century) in *The Age of the Saints in the Early Celtic Church* (Felinfach: Llanerch Publishers [1960] [Facsimile Reprint]).

Chiovaro, F., 'Cassian, John (Johannes Cassianus)', *New Catholic Encyclopedia* 3 (Washington: Catholic University of America/ Thomson-Gale, 2003), 205–7.

Evans, G., 'Deadly Sins' in M. Downey, ed., NDCS, 248–51.

Harrington, D.J., 'The Gospel According to Mark' in R.E. Brown, J.A. Fitzmyer, R.E. Murphy eds., *The New Jerome Biblical Commentary* (London: Geoffrey Chapman, 1990), 596–629.

Irwin, K.W., '*Lectio Divina*' in M. Downey, ed., NDCS, 596.

John-Paul II, Pope, *L'Osservatore Romano*, Rome, 2 Feb. 1988.

Schneiders, S., 'Spirituality in the Academy', *Theological Studies*, 50 (1989), 676–97.